Transforming
Bible
Study

Transforming
Bible
Study

SECOND EDITION
COMPLETELY REVISED & EXPANDED

Walter Wink

WIPF & STOCK · Eugene, Oregon

Wipf and Stock Publishers
199 W 8th Ave, Suite 3
Eugene, OR 97401

Transforming Bible Study
A Leader's Guide
By Wink, Walter
Copyright©1980 by Wink, Walter
ISBN 13: 978-1-60608-665-0
Publication date 7/15/2009
Previously published by Abingdon Press, 1980

To
Elizabeth Boyden Howes
with gratitude

Acknowledgments

For aid in conceiving this book, my deep appreciation to Elizabeth Boyden Howes, Sheila Moon, John Petroni, and Joan Gibbons of the Guild for Psychological Studies. Richard Griffis goaded and Dwayne Huebner guided its formation. The Arthur Vining Davis Foundations provided funds for field testing several drafts; and helpful feedback was provided by Amy Beveridge, Judith Grey Chendo, Marjorie Davis, E. Anne Eberle, Anne Flynn, W. Alan Gilburg, Douglas Lewis, Barbara Thain McNeel, Peter H. Meek, George A. Riggan, Sharon Ringe, Wayne Robinson, Martha Robson, J. Philip Swander, Kenneth Taylor, Patricia Van Ness, Lee D. Carey, Chet Copeland, Nan Merrill, and Eugene P. Wratchford. For unconscionable patience in typing various drafts, my thanks to Martha Robson, Sharon Abner, and Rosalee Maxwell. Adair Lummis provided an exhaustive evaluation of several Auburn Seminary workshops, thanks to the Davis Foundations. Caroline Usher, who did research funded by the same grant, plowed fields which I will be harvesting the rest of my life. A subsequent publication will, I hope, incorporate the returns from her excellent labor. Virginia Clifford and John Hendrickson of Auburn Seminary guided the project from inception to completion. Finally, my gratitude to the Arthur Vining Davis Foundations, for making so much possible which otherwise would not have happened.

Contents

Speaking of sacred texts, Heinrich Zimmer wrote:

"They are the everlasting oracles of life. They have to be questioned and consulted anew, with every age, each age approaching them with its own variety of ignorance and understanding, its own set of problems and its own inevitable questions. . . . The replies already given, therefore, cannot be made to serve us. The powers have to be consulted again directly—again, again, and again. Our primary task is to learn, not so much what they are said to have said, as how to approach them, evoke fresh speech from them, and understand that speech."

—*The King and the Corpse*

Preface to the Second Edition

A second edition is like a reprieve. One seldom has a chance to undo mistakes publicly made, or to expand on ideas too truncated or ill-developed, or to note the large omissions that have glared, unforgiving, like unfed cats. Ten years of peripatetic workshops, repeated attempts to train others in this approach, and further developments in my own thinking have taught me much that I have now been able to incorporate into this book. My thanks to Paul N. Franklyn of Abingdon Press for proposing this revision and seeing it through publication.

At the time I drafted the first edition in 1979 I was already hard at work on what has ballooned into a three volume work on the principalities and powers (*Naming the Powers*, 1984; *Unmasking the Powers*, 1986; and *Engaging the Powers*, forthcoming). I had come to this approach to Bible study through the highly personal, introspective orientation of the Guild for Psychological Studies, and most of my questions and exercises focused on the transformation of individuals. I was wanting to find ways to add to that emphasis a more balanced perspective on social transformation. But it is not easy to tackle the political implications of Scripture in our Western culture, for our whole ideology is undergirded by individualism. We think psychologically, not sociologically. Whenever we encounter injustice, we attempt to individualize it. The victim must be at fault, or some morally corrupt person in the system. We seldom address the systems themselves. They are, for many people, virtually invisible.[1]

I have therefore now included questions for a number of passages on the principalities and powers. But it is not a matter of simply adding a question here and there, but of trying to build a whole alternative metaphor to counter individualism. I have attempted to do that through the concept of the Powers. I find that I am still unable to integrate that metaphor fully into this book. It is a massive cultural problem and will not yield easily. I have done what I could to integrate the social with the personal here, but there is much that remains to be done. I urge the reader to join me in the search for better ways to integrate these concerns, and to seek, in each study, or at least over a series of studies, to keep the personal and social in balance.

When I first used the right/left brain research as a way of picturing for the reader the value of a more wholistic approach, I was taking something of a gamble, because the field of bilateral brain research was relatively new, and continuing developments might easily have disconfirmed or outdated my report. My hunch was vindicated shortly after publication, however, when Roger W. Sperry, one of the pioneers of split brain research, was awarded the Nobel Prize in Medicine and Physiology in 1981. Further developments in the field have not fundamentally changed the data I had presented, but I have updated the chapter and added more recent bibliography.

Now, however, I face the opposite problem: right/left brain theory has become so popularized, oversimplified, one-sidedly interpreted, emptied of its subtlety, and trivialized, that the whole subject is threatened with banality. Misuse, however, is no grounds for abandoning such a helpful resource.

The most significant new development in my own work with this approach is the introduction of body movement as an integral part of our workshops. My wife, June Keener-Wink, now begins all our sessions with 45 minutes to an hour of relaxation, centering, meditation, stretching, and a whole series of simple movements that gradually enable participants to move freely and spontaneously, many for the first time in their lives. When we then turn to Scripture, the discussion moves at a far deeper level, free of the usual intellectual one-upsmanship and competition.

More fundamentally, people begin to realize that the goal of the Bible study is not merely understanding or even new insights, but incarnating the Word, enfleshing it, getting it into the substance of our living. Christianity has been unkind to the body; there has been a docetic rejection of the flesh, sexuality, sensuality, even of nature. This rejection becomes most poignant in the profound hatred many people feel toward their own bodies. A great deal of healing is needed in order to restore people to a sense of their bodies as the temple of the Holy Spirit.

June's work is too extensive to add to this book; for the time being one can only attend a workshop and/or buy a set of tapes of June's work, which can be ordered from Nancy Sugars, 66 Lincoln Ave., San Anselmo, CA 94960.

Training seminars in this approach are available through Auburn Seminary (3041 Broadway, New York, NY 10027), as is a schedule of our workshops. Auburn has also recently introduced an advanced seminar in Bible study leadership as well, for those who have been leading in this mode for some time. If there is any way we can be of help, please let us know!

This is a "how-to" book on Bible study. The approach (which I did not invent) is the most revolutionary and far-reaching in its implications of any I know about. So, while in one sense it is simply a how-to book, it is also a satchel bomb packed with high explosives. You can scarcely try this mode of group study without being forced to change. If you doubt that is the case, stop now! It is intended only for those who *want* to be transformed and to work toward transformation with others. Those who wish simply to pilfer easy skills should look elsewhere.

The approach is one that I have adapted from the Guild for Psychological Studies in San Francisco, California. Their basic seminars at Four Springs, the Guild's center near San Francisco, run for seventeen days and are enhanced both by the intensity that such a setting makes possible and by the healing *mana* that pervades the place. Their leaders are rigorously trained in biblical criticism and depth psychology, have submitted to a long apprenticeship and personal psychotherapy, and have committed themselves to their own religious journeys.

The approach described in this book, by contrast, is intended for use by laity or clergy in congregations, prisons, hospitals, and homes, in groups with limited time (a Sunday morning class, an evening series, a seminary or college class, a weekend retreat), with persons far more tentative in their commitment to transformation. Lacking the total environment, leisure for personal reflection, and adequate use of the arts to amplify the experience of the text, these local study groups cannot hope to reach the depth of involvement that one can experience at an extended seminar or at Four Springs. Nevertheless, the texts are so powerful and the need so profound that I have modified elements of the Guild's approach in order to make available something of the experience that Scripture studied in this way makes possible.

Whereas the Guild for Psychological Studies and I work in close collaboration and have mutually benefited from the exchange, the Guild has reservations about the manner in which the method should be disseminated. The Guild has not popularized its method because of the conviction that people who lead need to have had experience of the seminars. This applies to the seminar method and to particular nonverbal techniques described in chapter 8.

The basic rationale for this approach has already been worked out in *The Bible in Human Transformation* (Philadelphia: Fortress Press, 1973). Chapter 1 of the present work goes a step further, using "split-brain" theory to illustrate the importance of holding critical study and personal encounter with Scripture together in indissoluble unity. Some practical idea of how these two poles are kept in tandem is provided in the chapters that follow. Chapter 2 gives an overview of the process that a group experiences, while chapter 3 depicts a group in action by means of actual transcripts. Chapter 4 then analyzes the steps involved in group process, with suggestions to help the reader at all stages of leadership.

To teach in this mode requires that the leader also be in process of transformation. Therefore the next chapter, which treats of the leader's own needs, requires special attention. Additional material that should accompany the reading of this chapter is found in the Appendix.

The essays in the Appendix are also of critical importance to the practical task of developing and using questions, the theme of chapter 6. Special problems for the questioning approach are presented by biblical criticism, for while literary and historical data are essential, the leader will have to decide when and to what extent they are applicable. Chapter 7 suggests a variety of solutions. Chapter 8 then builds on the split-brain theory discussed in chapter 1 by suggesting ways to deepen the encounter with the text by activating the right side of the brain. Finally, having analyzed all the components, we are ready to look at the way all the parts fit into the whole, in the sample questions of chapter 9.

I have tried to make this handbook as practical as possible. No written account of an approach which is so personal and experiential, however, could possibly convey the full contours of what happens in actual groups. If you have not experienced the process firsthand, I can only urge you to find a way to do so. The purple columbine on the page is not the one that grows in the mountain glade.

Chapter 1

Transformed by the Renewal
of Our Minds

If thy right eye offend thee . . . (Matt. 5:29 KJV)

For years I had been looking for a way to heal the split between the academic study of the Scriptures and the issues of life. For it was the Bible's way of addressing me that had led me into biblical scholarship in the first place. The sharing of those life-shaking truths was the very vocation to which I had felt so unmistakably called. For a time my generation of scholars was able to light our lamps at the fading flames of what Barth and Bultmann had achieved. When we were on our own, however, it was back to academic scholarship-as-usual. Even our concern for "biblical theology" was largely academic; we assumed that pastors and laity could make the connections to their own lives. More disastrously, we assumed that the *ideas* were all that counted, all that had to be applied. So we were a little hurt, and considerably mystified, when a growing chorus of voices outside academia insisted that what we were doing was not addressing human existence.

It was not until I became a parish minister in southeast Texas, however, that I recognized how profound this split had become. There, faced with the need to speak meaningfully twice a week from the biblical tradition, I discovered how isolated scholars had become from the pressures of living, how little of what they found fit to say had any applicability to preaching, to counseling, to the human struggles of those who regarded the Bible as somehow the key to life.

This was the pattern: scholars to the one side—like musicians so enamored of technique that they only practice scales; clergy and laity to the other—like people who love music but are too busy to learn to play.

Those five years in the parish did not produce anything like a solution. I was two different people: a scholar engaged in pure research unsullied by the needs of parish life, and a pastor desperately seeking a judging and healing word to a blue-collar congregation in the throes of the civil rights struggle and the onset of the Vietnam war. Those years did, nevertheless, produce something perhaps even more important. I now knew the right question. It was not, as I was taught, What is the meaning of texts? It was rather, Why is what we say is the meaning of texts not meaningful to people living today?

In 1967 I returned to Union Theological Seminary where I had studied, now to teach. I found that I missed the life-and-death struggles of the parish—birth, marriage, disease, tragedy, death. But I found plenty of anguish in seminary as well—draft resistance, war protests, black economic development, the Columbia "bust." The need to bridge the gulf between classroom and crises was never greater. I could only throw threads across. My sense of the malaise grew deeper, and grew apace with an awareness of inner malaise as well. For all my research was not deepening my own life one whit. If anything, it was keeping life at bay. And the Bible itself, which had always been the greatest stimulus to my growth, was becoming increasingly sterile and remote. Something had to change. So I began a journey . . .

. . . Which took me at length to a seminar of the Guild for Psychological Studies in San Francisco. Directed there by two former students, David and Penny Mann, I found full blown and beyond the farthest reaches of my own conception the elements of my own experience that had been most meaningful, gathered with new insights into a total pattern of stunning integrity. I had gone to seminary in the first place because I wanted to be an instrument of God in the transformation of persons. At the time that I began the study of the New Testament I also entered Jungian therapy; the connections were immediately compelling. During that same period I was doing field work with a group of teen-agers in upper Manhattan. Tired of watching them drift off to sleep during my Sunday school lessons, I decided on the bus one morning to turn the whole lesson into questions and let them figure out their own answers. The result was startling. Over a period of two years I watched those street kids turn into rare human beings, because someone had believed they could find the truth for themselves. Those four strands—a commitment to transformation, a love for the New Testament, a sense of the value of Jungian psychology and of the questioning method—whose interconnections I had not developed further, had been woven together by Elizabeth Boyden Howes and her associates into an approach to human transformation through an inductive, questioning study of Scripture aided by insights drawn from Jungian psychology.

Do not let your left hand know what your right hand is doing. (Matt. 6:3)

So I arrived at my first Guild Seminar in 1971, full of expectation. I was eager to wrestle with the personal and social meaning of the Bible for today, but I was little prepared to be sent off to paint pictures of the baptism of Jesus or to move meditatively to music or to work in clay or hike trails reciting mantras or to beat drums or meditate on paintings. But I was game, and I tried, with embarrassment and a degree of that condescension of a biblical Ph.D. going along with the assignments. So that I was totally shocked when, for example, the real power of our study of the story of the healing of the paralytic hit me, not as we were discussing it, but when I attempted to internalize the story, to find the aspect of me that is "paralyzed" and has never taken its rightful role in my selfhood. I was instructed to make the "paralytic" in me in clay. But "I" didn't make it. It made itself. "I" had no paralytic. "I" was shocked. My hands made it and suddenly it was there before me—an almost totally atrophied feeling function of whose absence from my life I was only vaguely aware. I knew immediately that what my hand had made was a revelation from God about my own need for healing, even though moments before I had known nothing of its existence. But if asked, I would have denied I had any need for healing. I discovered to my wonder that the entire body is an instrument of consciousness, and needs to be involved in the struggle to integrate God-given insights prompted by Scripture into the total self.

Very little in my previous training had prepared me for this. My capacity to feel my way into the text was almost nonexistent. I was not even equipped at the most fundamental personal level. For months, I kept in my pocket a piece of paper on which I wrote every day what I had felt. Often I could write only one thing. More often, nothing. Asked how I felt when my feelings were hurt, I would begin, "Well, I *think* . . . ." Learning to approach scripture in this way has necessarily involved for me a long, slow, and at times painful process of recovering lost functions of my self. But it has also been the most fruitful and exciting journey of my life.

One need not understand *why* something works for it to work, of course. Nevertheless I found myself casting about for an adequate explanation of the power of such encounters with scripture. Why had God been able to reach depths of my being through clay that had seldom been approached by careful exegesis? How was I to explain to myself, to say nothing of skeptical others, why I had been moved in such a transformative, healing way by something so simple, so—childish!—as this?

There the question remained, as gradually one piece of an answer and than another fell into place. I say "an answer"—I mean only a descriptive evocation, an approach to a mystery. I share it because I have found it to make sense of so many pieces of the puzzle of my experience.

The clue lies, it seems to me, in the physiology of the brain. For the very split I had experienced between the academic study of the Bible and my almost visceral encounter with it through clay is virtually mirrored in the way the two hemispheres of the brain are specialized.

Much of what we know about these two hemispheres of the brain comes from studies pioneered by Roger W. Sperry with persons in whom the *corpus callosum,* that bundle of fibers which connects the right and left hemispheres, has been surgically severed for medical reasons. The operation, called a cerebral commissurotomy, was first performed to relieve severe epilepsy. A short time after surgery the patients appeared to function normally, but ingeniously devised tests revealed striking changes. For example, if a person in whom the *corpus callosum* and the related commissures had been severed was asked to put her hands under a table, where sight could not be of aid, and a fork was placed in her left hand (the left hand being dominated by the right side of the brain), she would know how to *use* it, but could not tell its name. When the fork was placed in her right hand (the side controlled by the left side of the brain), she could tell its *name* but could not use it.[1]

Such studies have led researchers to conclude that the left hemisphere, which dominates the right side of the body, normally specializes in temporal and causal relations, speech, logical analysis, and verbal behavior. It handles grammar, naming, and abstract thinking, and processes information sequentially in a linear, orderly fashion. The left hemisphere is more adept at fine control of the hands and the vocal tract (hence speech). Its paired opposite, the right hemisphere, which normally dominates the left side of the body, handles spatial relations, gestalts, the synthesis of wholes, the grasping of meaning-in-context. It perceives shapes, sizes, textures, colors, and may be the center most active in meditation, dreaming, ESP, imaging, depth perception, complex visual patterns, and the recognition of melodies (among those not trained in music). It processes information more diffusely and indirectly, integrating material in a simultaneous, holistic manner.

The right brain tends to produce gestures with both hands, lends emotional quality to the voice and to facial expressions, creates new combinations of ideas by juxtaposing unlikely elements or comparing one element with another, and sees patterns and structures. It has no sense of clock time (*chronos*); it dwells in the eternal now (*kairos*).

The right hemisphere relates to the external world through vision, touch, and movement. It has the ability to visualize a complex route or to find a path through a maze, to generate mental maps, rotate images, and conceptualize mechanical contraptions.[2] Some people display different preferences in methods for learning second languages; rule learning or deductive methods correspond to left hemisphere strategies, and experimental-immersion or inductive methods correspond to right hemisphere strategies. The right brain is incapable of step-by-step procedures for solving problems or accomplishing some end. It does not seem to benefit from partial solutions, and appears to have a different concept of error or truth than the left hemisphere: the right brain finds truth in coherence, the left in correspondence. And, contrary to expectations, the disconnected right hemisphere professes more traditional, socially accepted norms. "It behaves more like the seat of the superego than the seat of the id."[3]

It would appear then from this information that the right hemisphere makes a rather decisive contribution to such activities as the visual arts, crafts, singing, and dance, and is the center most involved in intuition, visualization, fantasy, reverie, and metaphorical thinking.[4] The left hemisphere, on the other hand, seems to build up a hierarchy of categories for evaluating and judging reality. It identifies, classifies, analyzes, describes, explains, and reasons. (See Fig. 1.) Both hemispheres can *understand* language, but the left is far more active in the production of speech. In normal people, whose brains have not been split by surgery, both sides function in extraordinarily complex interaction. Each hemisphere has a wide range of cognitive capacities and can handle a variety of behaviors, including some that would be better performed by the other hemisphere. So it is a matter of relative specialization along a continuum, not a sharp polarity.

But in most moderns, especially men, the left brain has been favored from childhood, so that our access to the right brain is to some degree impaired or unconscious. We don't feel; we cannot cry; we don't remember dreams. We can't draw or paint. We lack sensitivity. We don't trust our intuitions. We have trouble being present in the moment, or sensing the beauty around us. Our bodies are inhibited in any but culturally acceptable movements. We are, in short, Western males—and some females too (though women tend to develop with a lesser degree of functional hemispheric asymmetry, that is to say, they tend to be less one-sided—as do some left-handed people[5]).

The price we pay for this left-brain overspecialization is splitness. We tend to value only the processes and products of the left hemisphere, and to damn or dismiss or be puzzled by the processes and products of the right, and those who exercise it. Until very recently, for example, many scientists spoke of the left hemisphere as "dominant" and the right as "inferior"—a selection of language already biased in favor of the left hemisphere.

Recent commissurotomy (or split-brain) studies have shown that the two disconnected hemispheres, working on the same task, may process the same sensory information in distinctly different ways. The two modes of mental operation, in which the right brain features spatial synthesis and the left features temporal analysis, can actually lead to mutual antagonism within the same body. One male patient whose two hemispheres had been severed was given several wooden shapes to arrange to match a certain design. His attempts with his right hand (left hemisphere) failed repeatedly. His right hemisphere kept trying to help, but whenever it did, the right hand would knock the left hand away. Finally the man had to *sit* on his left hand to keep it away from the puzzle. When the researchers suggested that he use both hands, the spatially "smart" left hand had to shove the spatially "dumb" right hand away to keep it from interfering.[6] On another occasion, a split-brain patient who was angry at his wife threatened her with his left hand while his right hand tried to come to her rescue and bring the belligerent hand under control.[7]

That split sounds strikingly similar to the split I had observed in myself and so many of my associates, between exegesis and application, intellect and emotions, scholar and believer. We had been subjected to the academic and societal equivalent of a cerebral commissurotomy!

Now it was clear why even the most lucid, trenchant, and precise scholarly studies seldom moved people to change: such studies were being allowed access to only a fraction of the self. They were not involved in a total encounter with people's lives.

In his right mind (Mark 5:15)

Enter the positive value of brain research. For every indication from this fledgling but solid science suggests that

LEFT HEMISPHERE
(facing away)

Dominates the right side
of the body

Temporal relations
Linear time sense (*chronos*)
Thinking: Analytical
           Logical
           Abstract
           Sequential
           Cause and Effect
           Digital
Speech
Grammar
Naming
Music (trained)

Figure 1

RIGHT HEMISPHERE
(facing away)

Dominates the left side
of the body

Spatial relations
Simultaneous time sense
  (kairos)
Thinking: Synthetic
            Imaginative
            Holistic
            A-causal
            Metaphorical
Art: Music (untrained)
       Copying designs
       Depth Perception
       Complex visual patterns
Recognition of faces
Gestures and facial
  expressions
Vocal timbre
Voice recognition
Gestalts
Shapes, sizes, colors,
  textures, forms

the brain itself was not meant to function by using only the left hemisphere. It is specialized, but not compartmentalized, and anyone who wishes to use the whole brain will have to enlist, sooner or later, the less used side. Musicians are a case in point. Those of us who enjoy music but are not trained in it will most likely recognize melodies with the right hemisphere. But those who are musicians will be busy analyzing with their left.[8] In the process of becoming trained, however, the musician may lose the capacity for sheer abandonment to the beauty of music without feeling compelled to name the piece, analyze the composition, or critique the performance. It is the Midas touch. Musicians, like biblical scholars, have to struggle to that "second naïveté," as Paul Ricoeur calls it, where we enjoy both analytically and synthetically the total impact of the score or text on the self—and that means learning to employ both hemispheres.

The researchers conclude:

> It seems unequivocal, then, that the left and right modes of functioning are not independent in the intact brain. Rather, it is likely that hemispheric functions are highly integrated and the relative contributions of each side to a task are dependent upon the demands of a situation and the differential capacities of the hemispheres within a particular individual.[9]

Another study, performed at the Mead School, asked what would happen to math scores if students up through the sixth grade studied *less* math and increased their work in art and music to 50 percent of the curriculum.[10] The result: Math scores went *up*! Why? Is it because, when students steeped in art turned to math, they were able to bring more of their brains to the task—especially that intuitive sense so essential to "hunching" one's way to a solution of a problem?

Do you catch the drift? We exegetes and theologians and pastors and people haven't been using *enough* of our brains when we encounter the Bible. We have gone as far as we can in one type of specialization—that of the left side of the brain—and now are literally threatened with extinction spiritually, ecologically, politically, and personally. Despite all our analytical lucidity we have lost the means to comprehend the purpose and harmoniousness of the whole and of our place in it—*a comprehension of which we are capable only when our right hemispheres are involved.*

One brain researcher, Albert Rothenberg, suggests that we need to develop "Janusian thinking." Janus was the Roman god with two faces who looked and apprehended in two directions at once. Janusian thinking would then be "the capacity to conceive and utilize two or more opposite or contradictory ideas, concepts, or images simultaneously."[11] This capacity to live with the complementarity of contradictory elements and processes in the brain is in fact the very source of creativity, for creativity involves the capacity to allow a perceived contradiction to reach its very limits and then be reordered at a higher level of integration into a new whole. Such an accomplishment requires both sides of the brain. The left must arrange the contradictory data in a logical, rational, and analytic manner, so that the contradiction can be seen in all its intolerable reality. That requires the courage of the intellect. Then the right hemisphere goes to work, synthesizing all these disparate pieces into a higher unity. This is the testimony of almost all the great discoverers: they worked on the problem until every avenue was exhausted; then the solution came to them in a dream, a reverie or a flash of revelation. One thinks of Newton's "apple," or Watson's sudden apprehension of the double-helix structure of the DNA molecule, or Kekule's conceptualization of the benzine ring while sleeping before a fire. The essence of creativity, concludes Kenneth Pelletier, entails the synthesis of left and right hemisphere functions.

The same might be said for religious, mystical, or transcendental experiences. Eugene d'Aquili and Charles Laughlin studied peak or mystical experiences from the point of view of split-brain theory.[12] They noted that normal brain functioning involves a rapid oscillation from left to right to left hemisphere, from viewing the part to viewing the whole to viewing the part, and so on. From this alternation they hypothesized that the oceanic feeling of which so many mystics speak, that sense of oneness with all that is, and the conviction that one has experienced a reality more real than normal reality, is the result of sensory overload, when the "alternating current" of brain attention is hyperactivated, and there is a bridging or spillover from one hemisphere to the other, causing us to experience reality with both parts of the brain *simultaneously*. And that experience *is* more real than our usual sense of reality, for we normally are only able to see reality as whole *or* part. But in these rare moments we experience whole *and* part, form *and* content, space *and* time, feeling *and* logic, synthesis *and* analysis. We experience both modes of perception in a single ineffable moment, which can subsequently never be adequately described, since speech is primarily a function of the left hemisphere.

D'Aquili and Laughlin do not in the least suggest that the brain is the *source* of mystical experiences. They only maintain that the paths that such experiences take in the cerebral cortex can be charted thus. They speak (despite their title) not of the cause of such experiences, but of their effects. My point is simply that the mystical experience, like art and music—all of which have been devalued by many in our culture—are essential to full human being, and that now we can argue, in the very physiological and material terms in which they were formerly disparaged, for their indispensability.

It seems to me that we are on the verge of a significant step in human development, a transformation of evolutionary magnitude, in which the conscious recovery of our lost right-brain function has become a possibility—for good ends or for evil. (Yes, evil: the subliminal manipulation of consumers by advertisers; development of intuitive and psychic capacities for espionage; the danger of intellectual sloth and sloppy research in the name of wholistic impressionism.) One of the pioneers of the recovery of this dimension of the self was Carl Gustav Jung. As early as 1913-19, after his break with Freud, Jung withdrew from active publishing and public appearances and went through a time of deliberate but harrowing involution. During this period, he devoted himself to building a whole miniature city in stone and pebbles, to stone and wood carving, to painting mandalas, to dialoguing with inner wisdom figures like his famous Philemon. Anyone of less stature would have thought himself mad; Jung sometimes wondered. Out of this incubation was born his understanding of polarities, of masculine and feminine, animus and anima, and of the reality and power of the unconscious.[13]

It has long been the custom of psychologists to ignore Jung. It is hard to imagine that they will be able to continue to do so, for split-brain studies have now confirmed physiologically what he intuited during that difficult time. Jung believed that we are all masculine and feminine, a polarity of opposites, but that we have been culturally inhibited from living out one pole or the other. Men generally have less access to feelings, tears, sensitivity; women have often learned that intelligence does not pay, or that strength is unbecoming. Many people have experienced difficulty with Jung's terms "masculine" and "feminine," since they are so culturally conditioned. Men in Iran, for example, *do* cry, publicly and freely—and under the oppression of the Shah and the Ayatollahs they have had plenty to cry about! Brain theory may provide a more neutral language of left and right hemispheres for talking about what Jung called masculinity and femininity, avoiding the inevitable confusion of those terms with "maleness" and "femaleness." But what Jung had apprehended with such breathtaking courage during those arduous years is now being verified independently as implicit in the very structure of the brain.

With the weapons of righteousness for the right hand and for the left (II Cor. 6:7)

Truth would not be served if in our recoil from the one-sidedness of left-brain domination we plunged headlong and heedlessly into the right. That way lies real danger. Many today, especially intellectuals, having so long denied this other dimension, discover its voices and capitulate to them altogether. Others, predisposed to anti-intellectualism, are susceptible to the allure of a subjective, uncritical, uninformed exegesis, one capable of confirming them in their warm feelings about themselves, but having little power to renew their minds. It may be necessary for some of us to pass through a period of one-sided reaction in order to free ourselves from the tyranny of unthinking religiosity (by left-brain critical reflection) or of dogmatic intellectualism (by right-brain glossolalia, or by art and reverie, as in the case of Jung). But the task set before us is one of *integrating* the two parts of the brain, and the accomplishment of that task is immeasurably enhanced when we bring to it a religious commitment to our own transformation, whatever the cost.

It is not an easy possibility which is set before us. We fool ourselves if we believe that, simply because we favor the recovery of right-brain functioning, it is actually happening. We are no closer to a synthesis of the hemispheres when we learn that it is possible than before we knew it. I have frequently deceived myself into thinking that knowing the goal means I'm moving toward it.

There is even a risk in using split-brain theory as a metaphor for the religious task, since so much remains in this field to be learned.[14] But the metaphor has this important value: it can help to break that prejudice which favors all left-brain functions over those of the right. It can free us from the tyranny of omni-analytical thinking. It can whet our appetites for an encounter with lost aspects of ourselves. And it can restore a certain basic legitimacy to an entire dimension of reality largely denied existence by the modern worldview.

The case for encountering Scripture with our total selves does not rest on brain theory anyway; people have encountered Scripture thus in every age. I am simply using brain theory to suggest why such a total encounter is necessary, and to help the prospective leader understand that those exercises which are intended to evoke right hemispheric engagement with the text are not simply devices for "getting people involved," but are indispensable to the transformative process itself. Such exercises go far beyond asking what the text means to us; they "somaticize" the text—they cause the insights it fosters to be experienced as a "felt sense" within the body. If this feeling is lived with until it becomes objectified in art or act or articulated in words, the truth that the text bears has come a long way toward incarnation in our very flesh. And *that*, and not correct ideas or proper theologies, is what the text is all about.

This at least makes it clear why I can no longer content myself with exegesis in the current scholarly mode. It is *not* because I no longer find it valuable; it is very valuable indeed. But it simply does not use *enough* of the brain, the person, the self. Our problem is not that we have been too intellectual, but that we have been half-wits! There is nothing anti-critical or anti-intellectual about this approach; on the contrary, it simply seeks to enlarge our understanding of the range of the mind's powers. I want to see people transformed, which means, practically speaking, that new ideas about the text are not enough. We must get our whole selves involved with it, right brain as well, and struggle to let it endow us with a fuller share of our available humanity. Likewise, left-brain exegesis, taken in isolation, fails to grasp the full significance of the text *in its own right*, for the text is more than simply a left-brain creation. We must find ways to bring our *whole* selves to texts that are themselves the product of processes that involve both hemispheres.

For example, the Bible is full of metaphors, word pictures, parables, and word plays. These were served up by the right brain to their authors, and can only really be grasped by us when we bring our own right brains into play as well.[15] That same hemisphere can help us fathom the complex patterns of a whole, after our faithful left hemispheres have analyzed the parts. This is why the interpretation of Scripture can touch people at the most profound depth when it first moves through a careful analysis of the text, with all the analytical tools appropriate to the task, and then finds a way to grasp the whole and juxtapose it with aspects of our own lives at the affective level.

Sometimes these transformative insights—I would not hesitate to call them revelations—have come to people through written dialogues with figures from parables or stories, regarded as inner aspects of themselves. Sometimes they have come through mime or role play, painting or movement. Such insights cannot happen apart from careful analysis of Scripture, but careful analysis alone seldom gives birth to such illuminations.

Another reason for enlisting the additional aid of the right brain is that the left brain's vaunted rationality is easily perverted by dogmatism and a kind of mental arrogance that goes far beyond issues of character. It entails a fundamental weakness of the left brain when its mode of rationality is given dominance. Michael Gazzaniga and J. E. LeDoux developed an experiment with a split-brain patient who had a snow scene flashed to his right hemisphere and a chicken claw to the left. The patient then correctly chose a related picture of a snow shovel from a series of four cards with his left hand (acting for the right hemisphere), and a picture of a chicken from a series of four cards with his right hand (acting for the left hemisphere). He was then asked, "What did you see?" "I saw a claw and I picked the chicken," he replied, "and *you have to clean out the chicken shed with a shovel.*" His left brain had no awareness of the snow scene and simply *invented* a reason for the card showing the snow shovel.

> In trial after trial, we saw this kind of response. The left hemisphere could easily and accurately identify why it had picked the answer, and then subsequently, and without batting an eye, it would incorporate the right hemisphere's response into the framework. While we knew exactly why the right hemisphere had made its choice, the left hemisphere could merely guess. Yet, the left did not offer its suggestion in a guessing vein but rather as a statement of fact as to why that card had been picked.[16]

This astonishing result suggests how little our interpretations of reality may indeed correspond to it. We clearly distort reality when we favor intuition exclusively and deprive our analytical brain of a chance to teach us what it knows. Most intelligent people readily acknowledge that. What we in the West are now beginning to appreciate, as other cultures have always known, is the severe limitations of reason alone, deprived of the intuitive, synthetic gifts of the right brain. Yet we know from experience what happens when mere intellectuality is allowed to govern our foreign policy (Vietnam, the arms race), our universities and seminaries, and, more to the point here, biblical studies. Michael Polanyi was not being anti-intellectual, but exceedingly wise, when he commented that an excess of lucidity is the enemy of truth. The end of the world, remarked Thomas Merton, will be legal. It will also, we might add, be fully rational according to the mad dictates of a coldly analytical mind.

On a broader front, this experiment reveals how a philosophy like materialism or a psychology like behaviorism, cut off from all the warm human feelings of value, love, and unity with all reality that are the right brain's domain, appears to the hypertrophied left hemisphere to be the only rational explanation for a world perceived from only an analytical point of view. And once the left hemisphere has been granted that ascendancy, it will only acknowledge its type of rationality as valid—all the while imposing its faulty view of reality on a human person whose right brain knows better but which, lacking speech, cannot argue back.

I will pray with the spirit and I will pray with the mind also (I Cor. 14:15)

Can it be that our development as fuller persons rides on our traversing that tiny bridge of the *corpus callosum,* thus bringing the two hemispheres into more harmonious communion? Is this not what the task of exegesis should really attempt—to move from unconscious fusion with our tradition, to left-brain analysis and criticism, and then, through a negation of left-brain dominance by evocation of the right, to effect a communion of left *and* right, analysis *and* synthesis, thinking *and* feeling, reason *and* tuition, in an encounter with the text by the total self?

Left-brain dominance, with its sense of individual distance and isolation from others, may have once been of value in a world less dense and infolded. Today, however, as Robert Ornstein has pointed out, what works for individual survival may work *against* survival of the race. Integration of right-brain consciousness with its sense of the interconnectedness of life might enable us to take those "selfless" steps which could begin to solve some of our collective problems.[17] With both hemispheres in synchronous unity, we might be less inclined to purely competitive modes of relationships, and more aware of the unity of humanity and its oneness with the whole cosmos and its source.

If God is indeed known through intellect and intuition alike, by logic *and* by revelation, then the long hiatus between science and religion, reason and the arts, mathematics and mysticism can begin to mend. Early signs of this healing are already clear in every area of society. It is my contention that the Bible can not only be rescued from the sterility of a pan-analytic approach by these developments, but can itself play a crucial role in the recovery of that fuller humanity which is our birthright and promise.

It is one thing to recognize the need for a holistic approach to the encounter with Scripture. It is quite another thing, however, to find a way to do it, or, having found a way, to master it. For the split we seek to heal runs not just through our training but through ourselves. To learn to heal that split in others requires that we be healed as well. The chapters that follow attempt to describe one such way. Perhaps as we attempt to employ it, our own needed healing will come.

Chapter 2

Introducing This Approach

Getting Started

Let us suppose that we are ready to encounter Scripture with our whole selves, and have joined ourselves with others at least tentatively prepared to do so. We have come together in a classroom, church, prison, living room, retreat center, or office. There are perhaps six to twenty of us—more people would restrict everyone's becoming involved, fewer would restrict the available experience and insights that can be shared. We begin with a time of silence for "centering," the leader perhaps bidding others to explore whatever anxieties they bring with them, whether they can be willing to let something new happen, whether they can be open to the Spirit of God as it speaks to us through the text, one another, and in our own hearts.

All participants have copies of the text to be studied—ideally, copies of a synopsis of the Gospels,[1] or a variety of versions of the New Testament. A passage of Scripture is read—I focus most often on the life and teaching of Jesus, but it could be any passage—and the leader initiates discussion by means of a carefully prepared sequence of questions that seek to enter the heart of the reality which initially gave rise to the text. The dialogue is, loosely speaking, "Socratic" or inductive—though in one essential respect it is not Socratic at all, since the object of the dialogue is not primarily a recollection of "the way we were" (*anamnesis*), but a discovery of the meaning of these objectively given texts for our lives. We begin by trying to understand the text in its own right, as an alien speech. Only when we have understood it in its own terms do we move to the impact of the text on us. Then, like that amazing television camera that can be inserted in a vein in the arm and threaded all the way into the heart to survey possible damage there, the text becomes a probe into the mystery of our own emergent but arrested selfhood.

We try to come to these sometimes overfamiliar Scriptures as if for the first time, unencumbered by preconceptions as to their meaning. We consciously attempt to adopt what in Zen is called a "beginner's mind." Since the leader's questions, if carefully prepared, have arisen from the very structure and intent of the text itself, we can trust them to help its meaning emerge. But we must apply our entire selves to the dialogue. The leader must also be alert to other questions which spring from the group, so as to flow with the discussion while at the same time adhering to the structure given by the text.

> The questions *arise* from the material and at the same time lead the individuals back *into* it. Correspondences or resonances between text and the individuals are evoked at various levels. In these moments something about the unknown is revealed. When the text is illuminated this way, the participants, too, in varying degrees, are illuminated. Meaning for individuals, not consensus, is the hoped-for outcome.[2]

When participants take responsibility for discovering the linkages between the text and their own experience, rather than passively deferring to "experts" to tell them what to believe, they begin to become aware of a new sense of personal authority and capability as agents in history. Gaining this ability to make conscious choices is indispensable for genuine spiritual growth. Part of the excitement in leading in this manner comes from watching people who had written themselves off gradually becoming aware that they are able to make profound statements, speak meaningfully to others' lives, and be personally in touch with that Spirit which itself inspired the texts. They discover powers of discernment in themselves that they had never dreamed existed. They find themselves articulate where before they had been silent and afraid. Where previously they had accepted their lot in life as a kind of fate willed by a remote and judgmental God, they now find themselves becoming conscious, choosing human beings, risking the chance of becoming themselves. Whereas they had formerly clung to the security of living by right answers, they begin to trust that they can live out of the right questions. Rather than docilely conforming to religious or social norms, they find themselves struggling to discover what God wants them to be and do in the ambiguous flux of events. Instead of sheep blindly following a shepherd, they become conscious human beings on the road to maturity.

Setting the Group's Expectations

I usually lay down the following ground rules at the outset:

1. The text, and not the leader or the group, is the focus. The Scripture is like the center of a wheel, its spokes radiating out to individual participants. From this center both conscious and unconscious responses are aroused. Questions from the leader enable the participants to enter into dialogue with the meaning of the text at all levels—not just through thought, but also through feeling, intuition, even viscerally. Because this is a questioning approach, living with the questions is far more important than finding "right" answers. Most of us have been trained in religious and educational systems that teach that there is *one* right answer to every question. Not so in this approach. A really good question can have ten or fifteen good answers, all of them important for comprehending the text. If someone makes a perfectly brilliant statement and the leader continues to press the question, this is not because the statement is inadequate but because the reality is far too profound to be reducible to one or even all of our statements. This does not mean that "anything goes," but simply that the truth is like a multifaceted diamond—too brilliant, too exquisite, to be fully illuminated by a single source of light. Likewise the leader will not "approve" or "disapprove" of answers, unless they are factually in error. Participants are free to judge for themselves what furthers understanding and what does not. Debate is out of place, therefore, since it usually leads to a power struggle between egos, not a quest for shared truth.

2. Because we seek insights and not just information, it is essential that everyone join in the discussion; for insights,

which are generally born of an inchoate hunch or feeling, mature and become accessible only when they are articulated and shared. Sharing also objectifies the insight, and becomes a kind of commitment to attempt to integrate it into our lives. Those who tend to speak a lot in groups will need to watch themselves to be sure they are not using more than their share of the time, and those who tend to be timid and shy about speaking out in groups need to take responsibility for carrying their fair share of the load.

3. Some will have extensive background in biblical study. Others will have next to none. Nevertheless we are all equals before the text, for in regard to our own experience we are all experts. And since it is the intersection of text with experience which evokes insights, no one need feel disadvantaged. In fact, those who know most may have the greatest difficulty achieving a "beginner's mind," and thus be least able to let the new possibilities for selfhood emerge.

The Three Elements of Discussion

That is usually enough to say to set the stage for dialogue. In most cases the dialogue itself involves three components: critical issues, amplification, and application exercises. The first element, matters of literary and historical criticism, can often be minimized in a short-term study, if it is not crucial for an understanding of the texts chosen. A longer-term study of the Synoptic Gospels, however, should begin with some introduction to the synoptic problem (see chapter 7). Most critical material can be surfaced by questions, but if no one present can provide answers, the leader may have to provide them. But mini-lectures should be avoided, since they throw participants back into a mode of passive dependency. When information must be brought in by the leader, it can immediately be made the basis of a new question.

In any case, it is essential that the text be given its due. The value of the critical method is that it defends the text from our projecting on it our own biases, theologies, and presuppositions. It preserves the right of the text to be different from what we want, even to be offensive. If we are interested in being transformed, and not simply confirmed in what we already know, the critical approach is indispensable, despite the danger of shallow intellectualizing and the tendency to avoid personal and social implications.

The second aspect is amplification, where we try to live into the narrative until it becomes vivid for us. We attempt to reenter the matrix out of which it was created. We imaginatively slip into the skins of the characters of the story, perhaps by role play or miming, or by meditatively identifying with one or more characters. We explore the logic of the story or probe our understanding for apprehension of the meaning of the symbols, images, or metaphors employed. *Only as the text comes alive for us can we attempt to hear again the question that occasioned the answer provided by the text.*

There is a third and crucial element, the application exercises. This is the moment when the contemporary relevance of the passage comes to light, when we apply it to our own lives, our need for personal and social transformation. It is not enough to understand the text intellectually, or to see certain parallels with our own condition. We need to let it move deeply within us. By music, movement, painting, sculpting, written dialogues, small-group sharing, we can allow the text to unearth that part of our personal and social existence which it calls forth to be healed, forgiven, made new. It is easiest to back off right here where the payoff comes, to pull our punch just when the opening is provided. There is no way to convince anyone who has not gone all the way through the process that this ingredient is necessary, and it is all too easy for the leader to back off in the face of group resistance. Nevertheless it is essential for the full impact of the text to be honored. It is important to stress, however, that all such exercises must be integrally related to the central thrust of the text and arise from it. Gimmicks, busywork, or human relations exercises which are just tacked on without any essential connection to the study will be instantly sensed as inappropriate and rightly resisted.

Each of these elements will be examined in more detail in subsequent chapters. For now it is enough simply to note them, and watch for the way they are interwoven in the transcripts in the following chapter.

Honoring the Text

A word of warning is appropriate at this stage, however. The goal of this study is not merely subjective. We are not just interested in getting people turned on by, illuminated by, or even transformed by Scripture. We are first of all interested in discovering what Scripture has to say in its own right. Unlike those who practice a more subjective type of Bible study, focusing almost entirely on the impact of the text on life today, we are less sure that the biblical territory is "known." It appears to us as more of a *terra incognita,* unexplored wilderness, of which even the leader is largely ignorant. The concerted efforts of the entire group must therefore be enlisted in order to comb it for its treasures.

Most especially, we are interested in Jesus, not just his teaching but how he discovered it, lived it, made it the very pattern of his flesh. We are working from more than a hunch that in Jesus' way of relating to God, in his understanding of human existence, in what he has to say to us about finding life, something qualitatively new emerged on the human scene. Before the church made him the Source, how was he related to the Source? Before he was worshiped as God incarnate, how did he struggle to incarnate God? Before he became identified as the source of all healing, how did he relate to, and teach his disciples to relate to, the healing Source? Before forgiveness became a function solely of his cross, how did he understand people to have been forgiven? Before Jesus was made the only-begotten Son of God, what did he mean by calling God "Abba" ("Daddy"), and instructing his disciples to do so as well? Before the Kingdom became a compensatory afterlife or a future utopia adorned with all the political trappings that Jesus so resolutely rejected, what did he mean by the Kingdom? Before the church began to expect Jesus to return on clouds of glory, what did Jesus expect? Before he became identified as the Messiah (a role which critical scholars are fairly certain Jesus never ascribed to himself), how did Jesus relate to the profound meaning moving in the messianic image? Before "Son of man" became synonymous with all the other christological titles, to what did Jesus refer by that enigmatic phrase?

In short, before Jesus was taken up into the Christian myth, with all the incomparable riches that flowed from that, how did Jesus relate to his own myth: the inner unfolding of his own being?

Not everyone will have the interest or the courage to take these matters up. But one can scarcely rub against Jesus' life or teachings and not walk away with a patch of glowing phosphorescence. Every word he uttered participated integrally in the reality out of which he lived. Those major questions cannot forever be ducked, if for no other reason than that they were in some sense Jesus' own questions, and are embedded in the statements that he uttered.

That is why a subjective appropriation of meaning-for-ourselves is not enough: there is a dimension of reality here buried under the detritus of centuries, like a spring under an avalanche. When we rediscover the questions that have themselves evoked the text, and follow them back to their source; when we enter into the shared struggle to comprehend what is moving in the question, and bring to it not only the left brain—the thinking, choosing, rational part of the self—but also the right brain, including the intuitive and emotional and imaginative aspects of the psyche; when we are willing to suspend our favorite beliefs (and disbeliefs), our most cherished convictions and our most authoritative doctrines, in order to listen for what might be speaking to us from the texts—then it sometimes happens that a spark leaps the gap: insights are ignited, insights that move more deeply than at the level of concepts or ideas, but are more foundational, drawing on the archetypal or mythical dimension of existence. These insights have the ring of authenticity. They seem to verify themselves as true. They are accompanied by strange stirrings in the self, as if a child of mysterious origin were suddenly about to be born. There is something quite beyond us going on here, something transcendent, something revelatory. Jesus was in touch with this dimension, spoke out of it, lived from it. That is why his words can so unswervingly ferry us to that realm.

Our goal then is so to move among these mighty texts that we are transformed. To be transformed, however, means more than simply to add something new to an old structure. It means to renovate the structure itself. The critical work helps free us from old preconceptions, no matter how useful they have been. It frees the text to speak in ways we are accustomed to not hearing. The process of amplifying the text allows it to enter us as an activating agent. The application exercises press us to see ourselves in its mirror, and to begin the process of changing. All three steps together, however, drive even deeper: to that lost dimension, that uncharted land, where our own true face is known, and where what God is and what living is are one.

Chapter 3

A Seminar Revisited

The transcripts presented in this chapter give some idea of how this approach works in actual practice. Missing, of course, are all the silences, hesitations, rushes of insight, laughter, gestures, facial expressions, tone, and tempo. The reader will have to supply all that, as well as distinguish the fundamentals of this approach from the peculiarities of my particular style.

Three sets of texts are treated: On Loving One's Enemy, On Judging, and On Anger. Their themes nicely interlock, and each helps to clarify the others. While I normally do all three together in a two-hour session, each could be made the basis of a shorter study.

On Loving One's Enemy[1]

Matthew 5:43-48	Luke 6:27-28, 32-36
43 "You have heard that it was said, 'You shall love your neighbor and hate your enemy.' [44]But I say to you, Love your enemies and pray for those who persecute you,[45] so that you may be sons of your Father who is in heaven; for he makes his sun rise on the evil and on the good, and sends rain on the just and on the unjust. [46]For if you love those who love you, what reward have you? Do not even the tax collectors do the same? [47]And if you salute only your brethren, what more are you doing than others? Do not even the Gentiles do the same?	27 "But I say to you that hear, Love your enemies, do good to those who hate you, [28]bless those who curse you, pray for those who abuse you. [32]If you love those who love you, what credit is that to you? For even sinners love those who love them. [33]And if you do good to those who do good to you, what credit is that to you? For even sinners do the same. [34]And if you lend to those from whom you hope to receive, what credit is that to you? Even sinners lend to sinners, to receive as much again, [35]But love your enemies, and do good, and lend,

⁴⁸"You, therefore, must be perfect, as your heavenly Father is perfect.

expecting nothing in return; and your reward will be great, and you will be sons of the Most High; for he is kind to the ungrateful and the selfish. ³⁶Be merciful, even as your Father is merciful.

In order to abbreviate the transcript, I have omitted several of the opening questions. For the full set of questions to all three passages, see chapter 9. The dialogue that follows took place during the closing years of the Vietnam war in a class on the Gospel of Mark at Union Theological Seminary (1974). L = Leader and R = Response.

L: *Why, according to Jesus, do we need to love our enemy?* If you look at someone as an external enemy, you internalize that fact that you hate them. Then hate for them starts to destroy you. So in that sense the outer enemy is internalized. By hating people you really destroy yourself.

R: I can really relate to that one. I remember back during the mining of Haiphong Harbor, when Nixon would come on TV I used to get a shovel and pretend like I was shoveling the stuff away—that would be my way of not being angry, that I could just make a joke of shoveling the manure as fast as it came out. But one time I remember distinctly going for a walk and feeling this incredible pain and anger blowing up inside of me and wondering if I maybe should forgive him—just really battling my hatred for that man and trying to get that anger out and start trying to look at Nixon as a human being, trying to be in some sense compassionate for why he could do that. It was as if that anger and that hatred of that other person was just right inside of me. The same kind of anger and hatred that he was showing and expressing in the mining of Haiphong was going on inside me. And that was the clearest I ever got to seeing that they were one.

R: You were mining Nixon.

R: Yeah.

L: *What happens when we love our enemy?*

R: I don't think that necessarily anything would happen to Nixon, but I think that incredible things would happen to me.

R: But it doesn't mean that the enemy stops being an enemy. If someone is really doing evil, I still hate what they are doing. You could say that to love your enemy is to love with all your hate as well. We can resist her evil or injustice without obliterating her as a person.

R: In one-to-one relationships with people we know, we tend to create the response that we expect. We sort of set up an energy field that elicits from other people that response. Usually it's unconscious so that we can't understand why things go bad, and to a very high degree we cause them to go bad because that's what we expect, anticipate, and create. In a sense that's what we want. And it's very hard to admit that. So that to the degree that we refuse to let the terms for our response be set by the other person or the situation and can exude a different kind of energy field, to that degree a new possibility is opened up.

R: I have to own the fact that I don't really want to love my enemies. I get a lot of mileage out of having enemies and hating them. And I also have a big investment in hating myself. For me to love my enemies would mean I would have to love parts of myself that are simply unacceptable, and I don't know if I'm ready for that.[2]

R: What hits me hardest in all this is that hatred is usually a reaction to fear, and that my hatred of my enemy is a way of giving that person a lot of power to define me.

R: The way I heard this as a kid, "Love your enemy" meant suppress your hatred, pretend to be loving. That locked the energy up and made me passive. When I hate someone, the hate has nowhere to go, so it turns in against my own self. It becomes an unceasing inner dialogue which preoccupies me and is really poisonous. I even get angry at myself for dwelling on it. Loving the enemy would mean freeing the energy to flow without consideration of the enemy or what the enemy might do. That is to say, it takes the initiative away from the enemy and enables us actually to be free to stand without being determined from the outside.

L: *Why then love our enemies?*

R: Because when I hate someone I hurt myself. I certainly don't hurt the other person. And when I love the other person, I am being more loving to myself.

L: Why then doesn't Jesus say, "Love your enemy and it won't knot up your stomach so much"? *What, according to Jesus, is the reason or ground for loving our enemies?*

R: God loves them.

R: It's so that we can be sons, and I suppose also daughters, of our Father who is in heaven.

L: *What is God like, according to Jesus?*

R: He loves us, his enemies.

L: *How do you really feel about the statement that God is kind to the ungrateful and the selfish?*

R: God just loves, period. I count on that. That's why I don't see any problem with it.[3]

R: And if God loves the ungrateful and the selfish, then that gives hope to me, because I'm ungrateful and selfish.

L: *Can you imagine a world in which God did cause the sun to shine only on the just?*

R: Yeah, then you could tell at a glance who was just and who was unjust. The righteous would be standing in spotlights of sun, and the others would each have a cloud over their heads.

L: The mechanics of working this out are so staggering that it immediately reduces to absurdity. *Yet isn't that exactly how we have gone about organizing the world? What are ways we have devised for distinguishing the just from the unjust, the good from the bad?*

R: By dress. You can tell at a glance whether or not a person is "in" or not.

R: Church membership.

R: Race. Blacks are out, whites are in.

R: Being born on the right side of the tracks. Having money.

R: You can even tell it by the way people speak.

R: Don't forget sex. Men have the edge over women.

R: Straights and gays.

L: When you think about it, we have constructed a social world in which the truth is systematically denied. And *the God that this world projects on the heavens is what kind of God? What kind of a God is in the psyche of most people—including large hunks of ourselves?*

R: It's a God who's hateful, vengeful, who is against some people and for some other people, who is for the good and against the bad.

R: This kind of God only loves those who love "him."

L: *So what is the new thing that Jesus is saying about God here, that goes beyond the ways we normally regard God?*

R: That God really does love everybody.

R: God even loves enemies.

R: The "good news" for me was when I discovered that God wasn't out to get me, to punish me. That that rejecting notion of God was a part of me, not God, and that I could begin to change in terms of the God that I now saw wasn't out to get me.

L: *What does it mean that God's not out to get you?*

R: It means I don't have to try to please or appease God anymore.

R: It's like the parent-child relationship. My children do things that irritate me, sometimes make me furious, but that doesn't affect my love. I love them no matter what they do.

R: Hate's not just a reaction, it's a strategy for maintaining our egocentricity. And if God is kind to the ungrateful and the selfish, then we're being asked to quit being the center of the universe where our egos are always so fragile and delicate and where we have all these sensors out ready to receive messages of threat and then to strike out with an atom bomb. But if we exist in a totality in which I'm only one part and this person's another part, and God's love encompasses us both equally, then it pulls the rug out from under my moral grounds for feeling justified in my hatred. It's because God is this way that it becomes possible for me to love my enemy.

L: *Let's look at Matthew 5:48 and Luke 6:36. Which do you think best sums up the point of the whole paragraph?*

R: Matthew's "Be perfect" doesn't seem possible to me. And I don't see how it connects up with what has just been said.

R: Luke's fits though. "Be merciful, even as your Father is merciful" says that we should also be kind to the ungrateful and the selfish, and love our enemies the way God loves us.

R: Where then does Matthew's "perfect" come from?

L: Good question. Does it help if I say that Jesus couldn't have said "perfect" even if he'd wanted to? Aramaic had no word for it. The Jews never even developed the conception. It's a Greek aesthetic notion: the perfect circle. Jesus probably used either a form of *shalem* or *tamim*, both of which convey the sense: whole, entire, complete, finished. It was Matthew who introduced the idea of perfection when he chose to use the Greek word *teleios*. *What has been the effect on you of the command, "Be ye therefore perfect"?*

R: It almost destroyed me. I really tried, tried desperately hard to be a perfect Christian. And it seemed like the harder I tried, the farther away I was. Now I'm trying to get out of that perfectionistic bag, but it's not easy.

R: It doesn't mean "Be morally flawless." It means "Be perfect in love, the way God is."

R: Why doesn't it make that clearer then, if that's what it means? The church in which I was raised certainly understood it moralistically.

L: *If we follow the clue in Luke's version of the ending, how else could Matthew's "perfect" be translated as a summation of the whole paragraph?*

R: You must be accepting, as God is accepting.

R: Be compassionate the way God is compassionate.

R: All-inclusive.

R: Understanding.

R: We have to be forgiving, as God forgives us.

R: We are to be all-encompassing in our love, as God is all-encompassing in loving each of us.

L: *When we try to be perfect, what is the motivation for doing so?*

R: To be saved. To earn God's love.

R: But that contradicts what this passage just said. God loves us regardless!

L: *And if we think we have to be perfect for God to love us, what do we do with our imperfections: our darkness, our wounds, our fantasies, our carefully hidden sins?*

R: We repress them.

R: Stuff it down into the unconscious.

L: *And then when we encounter another person who manifests such traits . . . . ?*

R: We lash out at them.

R: Or withdraw.

R: Or condemn them.

L: *By understanding this saying then as a demand for moral perfection, what have we done?*

R: Why, we've made it impossible to love our enemies! You can't love someone if you're unconsciously dumping all your self-hatred on them.

L: Isn't this a tremendous irony? We have taken the very saying which called us to an all-inclusive love that embraces even the enemy, and turned it into an injunction that makes it systematically impossible to do so!

   Now, can you get in touch with that "enemy" within you, the part of you you can't accept?

(The discussion continues with several other questions, but this is enough to give the flavor.)

On Judging⁴

(I begin, before someone reads the text aloud, by having the participants put down on a sheet of paper the name of an "enemy"—someone whom they hate, dislike, or are just irritated by. Under the name I ask them to list everything about that person they don't like, as rapidly as possible—just words or phrases. After all have finished, we set the list aside for the moment and turn to the text.)

Matthew 7:1-5

1 "Judge not, that you be not judged. ²For with the judgment you pronounce you will be judged, and the measure you give will be the measure you get. ³ Why do you see the speck that is in your brother's eye, but do not notice the log that is in your own eye? ⁴Or how can you say to your brother, 'Let me take the speck out of your eye,' when there is the log in your own eye? ⁵You hypocrite, first take the log out of your own eye, and then you will see clearly to take the speck out of your brother's eye.

Luke 6:37-38, 41-42

37 "Judge not, and you will not be judged; condemn not, and you will not be condemned; forgive, and you will be forgiven; ³⁸give, and it will be given to you; good measure, pressed down, shaken together, running over, will be put into your lap. For the measure you give will be the measure you get back. ⁴¹Why do you see the speck that is in your brother's eye, but do not notice the log that is in your own eye? ⁴²Or how can you say to your brother, 'Brother, let me take out the speck that is in your eye,' when you yourself do not see the log that is in your own eye? You hypocrite, first take the log out of your own eye, and then you will see clearly to take out the speck that is in your brother's eye."

L: *What is Jesus saying here about judging?*

R: Don't attempt to evaluate another's performance because you don't know where he's coming from.

L: *But is that really possible?*

R: We do judge, of course, but we can draw back and think, Well, I don't really know the whole situation.

R: But don't you have to evaluate people's performance when you're hiring, or trying to size up whether someone is trustworthy enough to handle your money?

R: This is one of those passages that bugs me a lot. Every time I read this one I am covered with guilt, because I judge all the time—and I don't see how you can avoid it.

L: *Is it saying that you should not judge? "Thou shalt not judge"—is that what it's saying?*

R: That's what the church has always heard.

R: Jesus himself tells us over and over in parables to judge which person is right. So it can't mean we're not to discriminate.

R: It's funny, I'd always heard that as a command to refrain from judgment. But I'm suddenly realizing that maybe that's not what's being said. It's more like, Be sure you know what you're getting into.

R: This astounds me. I always thought this said you shouldn't judge. And I could never abide this passage for that reason, because it's not true. You have to judge. And now I'm seeing that this may mean something else.

R: I don't hear it saying that you shouldn't evaluate, but only that if you do so, you should use the same standard for yourself as well.

L: *He's warning against what then?*

R: The double standard.

R: Judging others by tougher—or easier!—standards than you judge yourself.

R: I'm sorry, it seems to me that he *is* saying that we shouldn't judge. I just think he's wrong.

R: Isn't he calling for a kind of objectivity here, where you see yourself in the same light you see others?

R: If you're harsh on others, aren't you harsh on yourself—doesn't that sort of follow? Isn't that how we get paid back?

R: In the East they might say, What goes around comes around. There's a kind of karma to judgment.

R: For me it even works before the "What goes around comes around." For me, it's "What goes around was here to begin with." It's sort of the biblical way to see projection. I've begun to notice this, so that now when I judge others I now have to ask myself, What is there in me that I don't like in the other person?

L: Let's look at what Jesus has to say about projection here. *What is the relationship between the log and the splinter?*

R: That's really odd. We usually turn it around the other way—I have a speck, the other has a log—like when we say, "Well, I may not be perfect, but *that* guy is *really* bad."

R: It's like looking at a telephone pole lying on its side—at the near end it's a log, at the far end a speck—but it's the same pole you're seeing all the way!

R: It's because you feel dissatisfied with yourself that you tend to see something you don't like in others.

R: It's the reflection of yourself in someone else that makes you so judgmental toward them. Otherwise you'd be more compassionate or understanding perhaps.

R: Yeah, there has to be some kind of correlation, otherwise they wouldn't tick you off as much as they do.

L: *Take out the list you made of things you don't like about someone, and put your own name beside the other's name, and ask how many of the things you listed are also true of you. What are the raw numerical scores?*

(The scores in this group ranged from 100 percent to one out of nine. Occasionally someone will come up with no correlation at all.)

R: There are three things I *don't* like about the person I put down. Two of them are things I don't like about him, and hate in myself. The other is something that I don't have and he does, and I'm jealous of it. I wish I had it.

R: A group of us in our church are in a marriage enrichment course, and we talked about how men and women often project parts of themselves that are unconscious or undeveloped onto someone else, and "fall in love." We attach to that in other people which we have no contact with in ourselves. Like, men who have lost all awareness of their feelings tend to fall for feeling-type women. Or women who wish they were better at thinking will be attracted to thinking-type men. People who "fall in love" aren't then really in love; they are in love with their own reflection in the other person. To really love is to see *them,* not just some lost part of ourselves.

L: *What is the destructive side of projection?*

R: Well, if we tend to project on others everything that we don't know about ourselves, both the good and the bad possibilities in us, then as long as we remain unconscious about what we're doing, we're stuck. We simply can't grow. No matter how dedicated to God we may be.

R: When we act out on our projections, either with violent rage or infatuation, we can destroy other people.

R: Or ourselves.

L: *What does Jesus call the person who doesn't work with the speck?*

R: A hypocrite.

L: *So who is a hypocrite for Jesus?*

R: A person who judges others by a judgment they haven't first turned on themselves.

R: So the message here is that we shouldn't render judgment on someone else until the same judgment has been used as a searchlight on our own selves. If I would do that, it would help me with my self-righteous tendencies.

R: I don't want to see us internalizing this *whole* thing; working on our own projections doesn't mean we withdraw into ourselves and leave it there. There are situations which objectively *deserve* anger. Dealing with the projections could enable us to be really angry in ways that are appropriate, without having to go back and apologize later.

L: *Why is Jesus so concerned about clarity in seeing and being seen?*

R: If what we're about is doing God's will in a situation, then we won't be able to see it as objectively as we should unless we are working extraordinarily hard at being conscious of what we are bringing to the situation.

R: It's not enough then to be committed to doing God's will, not enough to have a good will toward God. God's work requires this hard work on ourselves.

L: *How did Jesus himself deal with other people's projections on him?*

R: He throws it right back on the rich young ruler: "Why do you call me good?"

L: *Now, relating all this to the previous passage, why do we need our enemies?*

R: *(In a sudden rush of insight)* In order to love ourselves!

R: That's it! God won't let us be saved apart from our enemies. We can't be whole without them.

L: *What can our enemy do for us that nobody else can do?*

R: Make us look at ourselves.

R: Be a mirror held up in front of us, to see what we couldn't see otherwise about ourselves. The kinds of things our friends either can't see or won't tell us.

R: So even if we do judge others unfairly, it can be turned into a healthy thing if we will *deal* with it, and learn to see who we are through the people we condemn.

R: And then we can also see to "take the speck out" of our brother's or sister's eye as well. I mean, Jesus is not saying, "Mind your own business." We need to live in relationships of mutual accountability. We need help in facing our faults. And if we can get our own logs out, we can really be helpful to others in getting theirs out as well, because we can now see it for what it is.

On Anger[5]

Matthew 5:21-24

21 "You have heard that it was said to the men of old, 'You shall not kill; and whoever kills shall be liable to judgment.'[22] But I say to you that every one who is angry with his brother shall be liable to judgment; whoever insults his brother shall be liable to the council, and whoever says, 'You fool!' shall be liable to the hell of fire.[23] So if you are offering your gift at the altar, and there remember that your brother has something against you, [24]leave your gift there before the altar and go; first be reconciled to your brother, and then come and offer your gift.

L: *What have been the consequences through Christian history of this injunction not to be angry?*

R: Guilt for not being able to live up to the commandment.

R: Holding back negative reactions. A feeling that it's wrong to be angry.

R: "Christians are nice people."

R: I'm not a nice person so I'm not a Christian.

L: *What has been your own personal history with this text?*

R: I hold the anger in till I explode.

R: I yell at my wife when what I'm really doing is displacing anger at someone at work.

R: Ulcers.

L: *How would it change the way you perceived this if we used the NEB's translation, "Anyone who* **nurses** *anger" must be brought to judgment"?* It's a present participle, indicating action continuous in the present, so it's a valid translation. *What images do you get when you think of* **nursing** *anger?*

R: Smoldering.

R: Hanging on to it.

R: Feeding it, justifying it.

R: Encouraging it along.

R: It's at the breast, it's taking in all this milk, it's growing, getting bigger and bigger.

L: *So we're doing what with the anger?*

R: Letting it eat us up. (*Laughter*)

L: *If we took that translation as our guide, then, Jesus might be suggesting that we deal with anger how?*

R: Don't carry it.

R: Don't let it suck you dry.

R: Don't nurture it.

L: *And the lines about not insulting or calling another "Fool" suggest what limits in the way we deal with it?*

R: You have to work with it in yourself first so that you don't blow up and cause something even worse.

L: Let's add to this text Ephesians 4:26-27. Someone read that in the RSV.

R: "Be angry but do not sin; do not let the sun go down on your anger, and give no opportunity to the devil."

L: *What is the writer saying here?*

R: Get it taken care of that day?

R: I'm intrigued by the last line—don't give the devil a chance, by letting the sun go down on your anger.

L: *Why does that give the devil a chance?*

R: It festers.

R: During the night it works on you unconsciously. Maybe it gets hooked up with the shadow side of your personality.

R: Are you saying that's of the devil? Could it be of God?

L: God can work with it, but only if it's raised to consciousness. If you leave it unconscious, the anger hooks into all sorts of other negative things inside and gives them energy. And you're already not conscious or you'd have been working with your anger.

R: The symbolism of sun and darkness seems to bear that out. Satan is always around, but only gets a chance if we don't deal with it.

L: *And the first clause of the Ephesians passage is in the imperative. What is it saying?*

R: *Be* angry. It's a command!

L: Isn't it curious how the church, with all the injunctions it has laid upon itself, has never seen this one. BE ANGRY. Notice how some other versions soften that to "If you are angry." *What does that do?*

R: That tells me it's really not permitted to be angry, that it's not an inevitable and essential part of my humanity, even good at times. It treats it as a moral failure which must not be allowed to lead to sinning against others.

L: It's amazing how poorly we Christians deal with anger. I suspect that it's even harder for many of us to come to terms with than sex. I still find it hard to *feel* anger even when I know I *ought* to, so deeply has it been driven underground. Now, back to the text in Matthew: "So if you are offering your gift at the altar, and there remember that your brother has something against you"—that's a little surprising, isn't it? *How would you have expected that to be worded?*

R: "If you have something against your brother."

L: *So why is it, "If your brother has something against you"?*

R: Normally if someone's mad at me, I feel it's their responsibility to initiate reconciliation.

R: But he's saying it's *our* responsibility! We have to take the initiative, even if it's not our fault.

R: I don't like that, but I can see the reasoning. Otherwise you might wait till hell freezes over for the other guy to apologize, and it's just not going to happen.

L: *And what is the content of "altar" for you?*

R: It signifies the presence of God.

R: It's a place of focus.

R: I have a comfortable leather chair in my living room where I sit every day and bring to God all the things in my life, including the disagreeable sides of myself. The altar says to me that God wants the whole me offered, not just the good and agreeable aspects. God wants my anger, and wants me to give it over to become what it needs to be. Anger is good, but it's just a start, like the initial explosion that fires an engine. Unless we bring it to the altar, it can't become transmuted into social passion, or forgiveness, or a more finely tuned, long-term, patient energy.

R: Yes, if we are *just* angry, and don't bring it to the altar, it becomes a huge energy drain that goes nowhere and produces nothing creative and may in fact become destructive.

L: *What is different because of going to the altar? How is the process of reconciliation going to be different because the altar is a part of it?*

R: Sometimes in taking it to the altar we are slowed down in our self-pity and the flow of energy out against the other and are forced to ask ourselves what *our* part in the matter was.

R: It prevents our trying to be reconciled out of an egocentric attitude. If we are still centered in ourselves, reconciliation isn't possible. We'll just open the whole issue up again.

R: If I've already worked through it internally, then *I* am different when I confront the other person.

R: The altar permits us to see objectively what's needed and to be reconciled with that. Whether others will accept it

too is not in our control. But we can at least maintain the
altar place within us.

L: *And why is it before the altar that this need for
reconciliation comes to awareness? Why there?*[6]

R: It's the place of sacrifice, where you go to establish
reconciliation or revive your relationship with God.

R: It introduces a third person into the situation. Now it's
not just how you feel or what you want to do. Now God
has a say in it.

R: And if we're going to ask for forgiveness, we have to be
willing to forgive others.

L: The "sanctuary" is also a place of refuge, where it's safe
for unconscious contents to "come up" and be dealt with.
It's curious that we don't come to the altar with this name
already in mind, but that it comes to us, as we're already
standing there, offering the "sacrifice."

Now, what I'd like to suggest is that we act this scene
out, each individually. Find a space somewhere and
make for yourself an imaginary or makeshift altar.
Actually visualize it as being in a certain spot. (If time
permits, have each person fashion a symbol that
represents wholeness for him or her as a part of the
altar.) Then physically walk through the act of bringing
your gift (real or imaginary) to the altar, and *there*
remember someone who has something against you, or,
if this is what comes to you, someone whom you have
something against. Leave the gift before the altar and go
to another part of your space, get two chairs, and place
them opposite each other. Sit in one chair and be
yourself; say what you need to say to the other person,
imagined as being in the other chair. Then sit in the other
person's chair and be that person, answering yourself as
that person might. You'll be amazed at how real their
answers will be. But don't just rehash the grievance.
Have a conversation that will actually move the
relationship toward reconciliation. We are trying deliberately to visualize and verbalize the actual possibility of
reconciliation. Keep moving back and forth from one
chair to the other till you have reached reconciliation, or

at least have gone as far in that direction as you can. Then go back to the altar and offer your gift. If chairs are not available, try standing in two different places. But by all means *change positions* as you change roles. Otherwise the dialogue will become hopelessly muddied. Take about twenty minutes, and then come back together.

(If space is limited, people can just spread out in sight of each other and do the exercise in silence, ignoring one another. Share afterward. If some people now feel that the next step is for them actually to initiate dialogue with the other person, they might contract with one other person in the group to do so within a certain time and to report back, as an added incentive not to put it off indefinitely.)

Chapter 4

Leading a Group

One of the most pressing questions raised by dialogues such as those in the preceding chapter is whether this leadership style is manipulative. Are the questions intended to elicit certain "right" answers? Does the leader have a goal or outcome which the group is intended to reach? For, in fact, questions do not just open an issue, they focus attention on a particular range of possibilities to the exclusion of others. And it is also true that the leader, by virtue of good preparation, has an idea where the payoff lies and *does* wish to lead the group there.

Does this process, then, lead to a genuinely open search for truth, or is it skewed toward certain expectations, responses, answers? That depends. If the leader still believes that there are "right" answers, the process will certainly be manipulative. If the leader has certain ideas that he or she is determined to work in by hook or crook, it will be manipulative. But if the leader has forsworn the need to control the mystery of life with "right" answers, and instead has learned to live by the right *questions*—questions profound enough to spend five years, ten years, a lifetime struggling with—it will not be manipulative. The leader is instead like a licensed trail guide who has been through these woods before, and knows some of the more interesting paths, as well as several dead ends. She can help us find some spots of scenic majesty, and can lead us to those verdant clearings where, in Heidegger's phrase, we can explore the mystery of being. The guide cannot make us see, or discover, or savor the wonders, but without some such guide we are likely to miss them altogether.

This model consequently places a rather high premium on the role of the leader. In a period when many, in righteous revolt against authoritarianism in all its forms, have abdicated their own quite legitimate authority as well, it may be necessary to remind ourselves that the word for authority in

Greek is *exousia: ek,* "out of," *ousia,* "being." One who speaks with authority speaks out of the reality which is itself being communicated, "out of being." A prepared leader is authorized by the group to *lead* them, not just monitor conversation. Yet the leader is no "authority," gives few answers, does not tell people what to believe or even try to garner a consensus. To put it differently, this mode of leadership requires a very high profile in the exercise of authority in terms of *process,* but a very low profile in terms of *content.* The leader, in fact, has been authorized by the group to empower members to become authorities themselves, to speak from their own experience to the truth they meet in the text. The leader dares not surrender that authority to the group, letting it veer off into a bull session at the first sign of resistance. Fortunately, since the text and not the leader is the real focus of attention, this approach avoids much of the counter-dependent behavior (i.e., "kill the leader") that leader-centered groups so often experience.

Let us use another image. The leader's function is like that of a conductor of an extemporaneous jazz ensemble at a jam session. The conductor does not know what a single member will play, but he must choose the key and keep the beat. There is a dynamic tension between discipline and spontaneity. And what is often true of art is also true here: the greater the discipline, the greater the spontaneous surge.

I have seen people discover together insights not one of them knew before entering the room. I have watched them meld into what I can only describe as a corporate brain, one person saying one thing and another building on it, and another on that, until together they have produced ideas they would never alone in all their lives have been able to think their way to—and which no exegete had previously discovered. When otherwise undistinguished people discover such unimaginable capacities in themselves and one another, the discovery is unhinging. They are not soon satisfied with any other approach.

An authoritarian personality will find this questioning approach unspeakably threatening. Even people who are genuinely open, who have not had training in this type of group process, will find it harder than meets the eye. Here then is a list of suggestions for developing or enhancing your skills as a leader.

Begin with a time for centering. This is to help people make a full transition into the group and to focus around the task of understanding the text and its meaning for us. I encourage people to relax, breathe deeply (and to continue to do so), and in a series of "bidding" statements, interspersed by ample silences, I invite them to bring themselves into focus around our common task, to be open to one another, and to be receptive to the Spirit as it speaks through the text, others, and our own depths. Sometimes I conclude this opening movement with a brief prayer.

. This is no "recipe," of course. I am sometimes amused in workshops when an ardent student is carefully copying down what I am saying as we are centering. These words need to come straight from one's intuitive sense and one's deepest commitment, and be born again at each utterance. I simply try to sense my own inner need and that of the group, and respond appropriately.

The use of such "bidding" statements is integral to the larger purpose. Rather than imposing my will on the group through a verbalized prayer, I find it far more congenial to invite them into an inner state conducive to our work together. "Can you let yourself completely arrive in this time and space?" "Can you be open to what the Spirit wants to say to you through the text, one another, and in your own heart?"—these are questions that make the leader's agenda clear without investing it with heavenly constraints, and place the burden of responsibility on each person to decide how fully she or he wishes to participate.

Ask for a volunteer to read aloud the text (or texts) to be studied. People could read silently, but having it read aloud places the text formally before the group. I would discourage calling on any particular person to read, however, or reading around the circle. A surprising number of people have reading problems, and could be embarrassed if put on the spot. Nor would I recommend calling on people by name to answer questions. Their participation must at every point be voluntary, in line with the stated objective of encouraging but not imposing their transformation. You may want to speak to certain members privately about their silence in the group, or challenge everyone collectively to join in more fully, but beyond that you must trust individuals to decide their own level of participation, even to the detriment of the total group experience.

Trust your questions. Discussion usually begins slowly. This is the moment of greatest peril, when the leader is tempted to give an answer to the question in the face of the silence of the group. Resist this temptation at all costs. If silence greets your question, repeat it. If more silence, repeat it again, or at most rephrase it. But *do not, under any conditions, begin giving answers to it.* To do so undermines the process. Participants sense your mistrust of the questions, consider it well-founded, and withdraw from your leadership. Your anxiety, communicated as self-doubt, makes them doubt that their involvement will be significant. Once you have assumed the role of answerer and expert, they will make you keep it. So whatever you do, stay with your questions. Generally, this is only a problem at the beginning, while people are feeling their way into the text and the group. They need time for that, so give them the silent spaces to find their place. Simple questions, related to data easily identified in the text, will encourage their involvement. As they gain confidence in their ability to discover answers for themselves, they will more easily tackle the really weighty questions when they come. You will learn to distinguish a full from an empty silence; let a full silence stand as a beautiful gift; in an empty silence, repeat your question.

As new questions arise in the group, try to orchestrate them into the central movement provided by your questions. But above all, trust your questions, and do not abandon them unless you are sure you were quite mistaken. And (to paraphrase Auden), if someone says, "You are mistaken"— they may be quite mistaken.

If someone brings up a question you plan to deal with later, either (a) deal with it now, or, if it interrupts another issue

inadequately discussed, (b) ask the person to hold it until the group can come back to it. But if you do delay consideration, always *be sure* you do come back to it. Otherwise it appears that you were simply sidetracking the question because you thought it unimportant.

Be aware of where you are in your series of questions, but don't let that prevent you from attending fully to what people are saying. If you are not fully present to people as they speak, they will read your preoccupation as a lack of interest or as disapproval; they will suspect that they are not giving you the answer you want, and you will miss what they have to offer.

When one or a few persons dominate, as is often the case, try to widen involvement as tactfully as possible. You might turn to others in the group and say, "We haven't heard from some of the rest of you . . ." (repeating the question), or, "Only a few people have carried the responsibility for the discussion. How about some of the rest of you?" Or you may simply have to ask someone not to dominate. You had better do it, though, or the whole process will be undermined, as people get angrier and angrier at the person involved.

A special problem is occasionally created by the presence of one or more hard-baked fundamentalists, whose response to the vacuum of uncertainty which your questions create is to try to fill the air with preconceived answers. Such persons will instantly intimidate others into silence or into giving what they think are "right" responses. A situation like this is best dealt with, one-to-one, after the session is over. Explain the presuppositions under which you are proceeding and invite the person to try functioning that way. Make clear that your goal is the transformation of persons in the group, and that for this to happen each must find the truth individually, in concert with others. In all this it is important to be clear in your own self that this person has a right to be a fundamentalist, as long as the rights of others are maintained as well. If such an appeal falls on deaf ears, then you may have to ask the person whether some other group might be more suitable.

If people begin debating with one another, try to encourage them simply to let their differences stand, without trying to force on one another a "correct" notion. Ask them if they can agree to disagree. Debate takes place when minds are already made up in advance. It is a power struggle to see who can impose his views on another. In this approach, on the contrary, the very presupposition is openness to the insights of others, even (or especially) when they are at odds with our own. For we grow as we encounter truths that cannot be integrated into our own understanding. Out of the tension created by the juxtaposition of two opposing truths, a higher synthesis may be born which does justice to both.

If things are not going "well," and you feel yourself beginning to press to try to *make* things happen, stop internally, relax your body, breathe deeply several times, and establish eye contact with the person who is speaking. By letting go of your need to control you may be able to flow with the process better. If that doesn't seem to help, or if you are encountering resistance in the group, ask people where they are, perhaps volunteering your own perception, such as, "My reading of the group is. . . . How do the rest of you perceive what is happening?"

Be sure that you leave time for the concluding exercise. Always plan your time backward, from whatever amount of time the closing activity will require, to the central section (amplifying the text), to the introductory critical comparisons, and so on. Be sure you don't let the clock run out before you have reached the payoff. At all costs resist the rationalization that runs: "Well, time is running out, and we've gotten lots of good, new insights into the text. It won't hurt if we just skip the closing activity."

Avoid talking too much. It can be helpful to keep reminding ourselves that we are not teachers but guides. We have to be willing to let people miss our most cherished insights for the sake of aiding them to develop their own. If you do want to help them see something, try to avoid making a statement; turn it into a question instead. Do you want to point out that Matthew's version of the voice at the baptism is different from Mark's or Luke's? Ask it as a question: How is Matthew's version of the voice at the baptism different from Mark's or Luke's? It is as simple as that! But it requires a whole new way of thinking. It is, of course, perfectly legitimate for the leader to make occasional personal contributions, but only *after* the group has been weaned from his or her authority as an expert. Otherwise they will be certain that you have given the one and only "correct" answer, and discussion will abruptly halt.

Try not to respond to each person's contribution, either by restating it or elaborating on what he or she has said. At first you may find all comments directed toward you. In time, group members will learn that you neither give approval nor desire to be the constant focus of attention, and will begin to respond more to one another, or out of a centered place in themselves.

When you have difficulty with a question, don't be afraid to acknowledge it. Sometimes you may have a hunch that some really profitable exploration could be opened up by a certain question, but when you ask it, no one "bites"—not that they don't give "the right answer," but simply that they fail to grasp the direction of inquiry. If you keep pressing your question, hoping that they will catch on, they may begin to suspect you have something up your sleeve. In such cases you can simply admit that you are having trouble, that you have a hunch that the group could profitably pursue the issue if you asked (here you rephrase your question) because (here you say what the connection is that evoked your question).

For example, suppose you have asked, in connection with Jewish attitudes regarding defilement or uncleanness, "Where does this fear of defilement come from?" The group may respond, "From the Old Testament," or, "From practices in the Temple." When you keep pressing the question they may begin to think you have the answer. At that point you might say: "No, I'm not asking what are the sources of the rules regulating defilement. I'm asking the generic question. I want to know what gave rise to the fear of defilement in the first place. Does that help clarify it?" Several members test their perception of the question: "The issue is not what *is* defilement but what causes people to feel that way—is that what you're getting at?" "Are you asking why the first person felt defiled?" That clears the way for the group to dig deeper, and you have avoided trying to give an answer of your own. (And anyone who thinks he knows the answer to *this* question is just kidding himself.)

Do not approve or disapprove of statements made in the group, unless they involve errors of fact. This lack of response is disconcerting to some people at first, who are accustomed to having been "graded" throughout their lives. Some are hurt when their brilliant statement is received without comment by the leader, as if neutrality were a kind of disapproval. An inexperienced leader might readily capitulate and begin feeding people's egos, unless it is clear from the outset that one of the goals is to break the very need for approval itself. If we are to help them stand on their own feet in their quest for truth, they simply have to outgrow the need for an external authority who can confirm their insights. Only as we learn to trust the authority of the truth which has come to us can we mature into fully responsible persons.

This does not mean that we no longer need the check of a community. Indeed, now the community can become a community of mature individuals for the first time, instead of a collective of peer-group pressures and dominant, authoritarian personalities. We can now safely test our insights against the shared wisdom and experience of the group—changing, modifying, strengthening, or scrapping them on the basis of others' comments—yet still knowing ourselves answerable for our own decision in the matter.

To some, however, a blank-faced leader who makes no response at all is disconcerting, and understandably so. Perhaps the leader might nod as speakers conclude, not so much in agreement as in encouragement, as if to say, "Yes, we're on the right track, let's work at this further," and turn to others in the circle for their comments.

Hold your ground. Resistance by members of the group or the group as a whole can take so many forms that it is difficult to generalize about it. You are bound to encounter it, however, because the material itself threatens our self-understanding, our lifestyles, our egocentric control of things. People are bound to react. They may do so by challenging the text, or the form your question has taken. You must be willing to hold your ground and not knuckle under here, for your role is to champion the integrity of the text against every attempt to water down, distort, or muzzle it. You can assure them that they don't have to agree with the text, but that in fairness to the text we need to let it say what it says.

Or they may challenge your leadership. If you already feel shaky and insecure, this can be devastating. But again, you must struggle for real objectivity and not just cave in at the first sign of opposition. Is the criticism, despite all its valid observations about your inadequacies (and who has none?), *really* aimed at dodging an arrow of truth flying at them from the text? Do they really wish *they* were the leader instead of you? We can't always know. But if you have prepared adequately, you have a right to ask the group to go along with you, and then give you feedback *at the end.*

I have done a perfectly miserable job of leading on occasion and have received a letter weeks later describing that lousy session as the turning point in someone's life. The Spirit can use even our poor efforts, and the knowledge of that helps get us out of the center of the picture and on the edge where we belong. But that also means that we should not take resistance too seriously until afterward. Comment on it, or bow your neck and plow through it, make light of it or encounter it with fierce determination—but stay on course unless you are quite sure you are on the wrong track. Then, when your work is finished, try to be as open to constructive criticism as you can, learning from your mistakes even as you make allowances for your critics' possible misapprehensions about the process.

Remember that people have a right not to be transformed. My experience suggests that the vast majority of people in churches are not there to be changed but to shore themselves up against the too-rapid changes of a souped-up society. Their metaphor is not the journey but the fortress. They will not be in the market for this kind of Bible study, and we need to be careful not to impose it on them. But if they have voluntarily joined the group, then take that as permission to work with their resistance. Recognize it as an inevitable element in the process of transformation, not as a menace to the success of your leadership.

Dealing with objections to careful study. Occasionally, someone will complain that we are poring over the text too minutely. After all, they may say, isn't this passage simply saying _____ (with which they reduce the text to a well-worn theological saw or moral platitude). Such an attitude kills all chance of hearing the text say something new. You might say so, or simply smile and forge ahead (unless the discussion has, in fact, bogged down; if so, move on to your next question).

Or someone may object to all this preoccupation with the actual words of the Gospels (for example) when they are English translations of Greek translations of lost Aramaic oral traditions, and when the four evangelists clearly felt free to change those traditions at will. All that is true. But since these texts are all that we have, we must treat them with the same respect that an archaeologist accords the scattered fragments unearthed at an ancient site. We regard Scripture with unashamed preference as a sacred text, not because it is beyond criticism or dispute, but because it has been the medium over millennia for the liberation, healing, judgment, and transformation of countless lives. We have no other option than to regard it with utmost seriousness, word for word, even when we do not like what it says. No other text in our culture has had a comparable effect. And despite the differences between them, each evangelist's story has its own integrity. Each word counts. It is the same with great music. Which note in Beethoven's Ninth Symphony would you want to change?

Avoid explaining one text by another. Samuel Sandmel aptly dubbed this process "parallelomania." It is of course very helpful at times to refer the reader to other parts of Scripture where similar issues are dealt with, or valuable background information is to be found. And in the final analysis no text can be understood in isolation from the work in which it appears and without reference to its relationship to the rest of the canon. But more often than not the tendency is to "explain" one passage by quoting another—which now must itself be explained. We are trying to think generically, back to the origins of things, and that movement is often not advanced by moving laterally to another text that simply articulates the same issue. Even if the group is in desperate need for as much exposure to Scripture as possible, which approach will best serve the building of a really solid foundation: driving one piling deep into bedrock, or gathering a mound of similarly shaped stones?

On the other hand, related texts can be extremely helpful. In "A Seminar Revisited," I used Eph. 4:26-27 to illuminate Matt. 5:21-24. But when a parallel text is used, be sure you take time to work with it also, for no text of Scripture should be assumed to be self-evident.

Don't be afraid of emotions. If someone bursts into tears, or is silently crying, and your intuition is that the material itself has evoked the feelings, simply be aware of it and go on. If the person seems to need support, it is hoped those nearby will provide it. Otherwise you will have to stop and provide it. (That has never happened to me, simply because people *won't* "break down" unless they sense that the group is supportive.) If the emotion seems not to have been evoked by the material, and the person can say where it's coming from, that will be helpful. On the whole, I regard the expression of feelings as a good sign. It can show great strength for a person to weep in a group (especially a man), so don't assume that people need or want comfort when they cry.

In addition to these specific points, here are a few general guidelines concerning this process.

It is usually best when you are starting up a group for the first time to do so for a limited period—four to ten sessions. Then if the group responds with enthusiasm, those who wish may choose to continue. It is most important, however, when you are gathering the group, to be clear about both the process and the goal, so that those who come have really contracted to struggle with the questions toward their own transformation. For that reason it is not wise to introduce this approach into a perennial Sunday school class, whose longevity as a group is more a factor of social considerations than commitment to individuation.

In order to start the group off with common expectations about the process to be employed, some leaders jot on a

blackboard or pass out a page of "ground rules" for group members, with comments about a searching attitude, not debating, participating, being honest, bringing their own experience to bear on the passage, openness and receptivity toward the views of others, the avoidance of stereotyped phraseology and religious cliches, and so forth. Make it brief, however. There are excellent samples in *Study Guide* for *The Choice Is Always Ours,* edited by Sadie M. Gregory, Elizabeth Boyden Howes, and Dorothy Berkley Phillips (The Guild for Psychological Studies, 2230 Divisadero, San Francisco, CA 94115), pp. 3-5; and in Mary C. Morrison's *Approaching the Gospels Together* (Wallingford, PA: Pendle Hill Publications, 1986), pp. 19-20. It would be best, however, if each leader developed her or his own list in order to adapt the approach to the specific needs of the local setting.

Group solidarity emerges only as individuals struggle to become authentic human beings. Our goal in working in this mode is personal and social transformation. Therefore the kind of group we seek is not one in which everyone feels warm and close, but one in which persons feel free to become themselves. Group-building exercises have only a minor role to play, beyond a bare minimum for introductions. We want to free people from depending on the group to "make" them what they are, so that they may freely choose to become themselves. Our desire is for a group made up of persons who have each solitarily gone through the "narrow gate" and are on their own hard way that leads to Life, not for that cloying kind of "participation mystique" in which everyone tries to be like everyone else. What issues from this approach is what Elizabeth Howes calls "the individual in community"— separate pillars supporting a common roof, not the collectivity of bees in a hive.

On the other hand, in order for trust and support to emerge organically from the common struggle to be addressed by what is moving in Scripture, it is important that there be continuity in attendance. Once the group has started, new people should normally not be added.

Does this approach work with other parts of the Bible besides the Gospels? Of course. It is most effective and easiest to do with narratives (myths, stories, parables), in which the Old Testament, the Gospels, and the Book of Acts abound. It works well with teachings or sayings that feature powerful metaphors, symbols, or images, as in the Prophets, Psalms, or the sayings of Jesus. It is even useful with the Letters of Paul, though sometimes more difficult, since Paul's writing is so very dense, discursive, and filled with mixed metaphors. The Guild for Psychological Studies has used this questioning approach to great effectiveness with such widely diverse texts as Mesoamerican and Native American myths, the *Gilgamesh Epic,* the Wagner "Ring" cycle of operas, and the Tolkien "Ring" trilogy.

Obviously, no one pedagogical technique is sufficient. I do not wish to propose this one as a panacea. Always seek to match the size and age of the group with the appropriate mode of communication, not restricting yourself to a single approach.

The same questions can be used with virtually any group, regardless of the educational or cultural background of participants. Clergy are especially prone to believe that they have to "simplify" questions for the laity, so accustomed are we to writing them off. It is my conviction, confirmed by seminars from East Harlem to Trinidad, from Westchester County to tiny rural communities, that people everywhere are equidistant from the ultimate questions of life, and that everyone is capable of speaking to them meaningfully through an encounter with Scripture.

Children also can benefit from this approach, though the questions must be simplified and fewer used. Children are marvelous at role plays and other activities. Most valuable for them, perhaps, is experiencing a pedagogical approach in which there is no single right answer, and which places a premium on their own creative thinking.

How might this approach affect preaching? First, in preparing the sermon, begin as suggested in chapter 6 by asking every question that comes to mind. Then organize research by seeking answers to your questions. This helps break the text down from a monolith of impenetrable granite to cut stones capable of being constructed into a sermon.

Second, if the texts to be preached were being studied in advance by a group in the congregation, sermons would be less idiosyncratic and more representative of the needs of the entire congregation; the minister would gain exegetical insights, some of which can be found in no commentary; and members of the group would listen to the sermon with new intensity, since they had an investment in developing it.

Having said that, let me add that we Protestants make too much of the sermon in the first place. Clergy egos are far too focused on it. There is in the sermon no feedback, no opportunity to find out where people are, or how the text is finding them out. The sermon tends to foster a binary form of left-brain response, a yes/no, I agree/disagree mode of passive assent or dissent, without provoking genuine thought or responsiveness. It perpetuates the clergy/laity split and the authoritarian image of the preacher as the sole dispenser of God's word. I have been in churches where there has been no Bible study in living memory. To grasp the enormity of that, imagine visiting a church where there had been no sermon in living memory. The Reformation ostensibly gave the Bible back to the people, only to see it spirited away once again by professional clergy and, later, by biblical scholars with their labyrinthine scientific apparatus. Good preaching can be an epochal event in the life of an individual. But if the renewal of persons that we seek involves their empowerment to discover God's will for their lives in community with others, then something more than monologue is required. Bible study is not just an emphasis to be recovered; it is a revolutionary possibility: whole congregations, broken down into smaller groups gathered to struggle together to decipher God's word for their lives.[1] Bible study is every bit as important as preaching; without it, preaching's centrality becomes a positive hazard.

This chapter has provided what I hope are useful hints about leading the group. But technique is not enough. Transformation, whenever it occurs, is a profound mystery. We do not know why it happens, or even how to make it happen. Methods certainly do not cause it, but they can facilitate or impede it. The role of medicine in healing is analogous. The salve I rub on my cut finger does nothing to cause healing; it merely kills bacteria that might prevent my healing. The healing itself, like our transformation, is an imponderable mystery, and is the very work of God. How the leader can participate in this same process is the subject to which we now turn.

Chapter 5

The Leader's Own Needs

The Leader's Transformation

The motto under which I work is emblazoned in this tale about Phillips Brooks, one of the great American preachers of the nineteenth century. A young apprentice preacher once complained to Brooks that nobody seemed to be affected by his neophyte attempts at preaching. Brooks responded, "You don't expect people to be changed *every* time you preach, do you?" The young man replied, "Why, of course not!" Brooks thundered at him, *"That's* your problem!"

If in this approach we make our conscious goal the transformation of persons toward the divine possibilities inherent in them, then we cannot be content with simply "having a good group," or helping people to "understand the Bible better," or "giving them more information," or even "trying to build fellowship." These are temptations to do the good, not the better. If nothing less than human transformation is our goal, then everything we do must be aimed at enabling people to become more precisely and fully the selves that they need to be in order to be available to God as effective agents of the Kingdom.

Transformation involves the movement from egocentric control of one's life toward a life centered on commitment to the will of God, whatever that might entail and however costly it might turn out to be. It is exploring all the sealed and stale rooms of this God's house we call our selves, and offering all we find to the real owner for forgiveness, acceptance, and healing. It is unmasking our complicity in systems and structures of society which violate people's lives, and becoming ready agents of justice. It is discovering the unjust and violated parts of ourselves as well. It is a process, not an arriving; we are "transforming," not transformed. But all along the way there are flashes of insight, moments of exquisite beauty, experiences of forgiveness and of being healed, reconciliations and revelations that confirm the rightness of our quest and whet our appetites for more.

Unless, as leaders, we ourselves are "on the way," and are struggling at the long, arduous, largely unseen task of integrating the lost or wounded parts of our own selves; unless we are fighting daily to silence the voice of our own inner "pharisee" and to affirm the divine word that declares us forgiven, loved, and accepted at the very heart of the universe; unless we are working at identifying the ways we project elements of ourselves onto others, and are claiming these back as lost aspects of ourselves; unless we are trying to alter our own lifestyles toward practices that are ecologically sound and economically just—then our leadership will hardly evoke these kinds of commitments in others. If we regard this approach as but one more skill to add to our arsenal of group dynamics techniques or parish programs, we will not only gut it of its most profound intent but deprive those whom we lead of any real chance for fundamental change.

It is not easy for many of us to give up our need for control, for having the right answer nailed down and accepted, for being looked to as the last word on religious matters. We may be restless with the groping and stumbling required to find our way into the text and back to ourselves again. We may find it difficult at first to believe (until it has happened to us again and again) that others with less training or intelligence have anything to teach us. For some of us who are pastors, even though we devoutly believe in the priesthood of all believers, there is a certain mortification required before we can allow ourselves to be genuinely the equals of our parishioners, to be ministered to by them and educated as to the meaning of these texts for our own lives. And for some who are laity, it may take genuine courage to step out in leadership without formal theological training, and a hunger for something more than simply a new way to make their contribution.

Transformation is not just something we are trying to provide for others. It must be our own deepest desire as well. We do not need to have arrived, but we do need to be on the journey. We do not need to have all the answers, but we do need to be living the questions. Personal individuation only emerges in the process of facing our own darkness, the parts of us identified by the Gospel stories as wounded, paralyzed, deviant, or withered, and loving them into the light of consciousness. It takes a great commitment to bring the many discordant strings of the self into the finest possible tuning, but anyone unwilling to make the attempt owes it to others not to undertake leading them—in this or any other mode.

Fortunately, the very act of leading involves disciplines which themselves can help further our own transformation. As we struggle to give preliminary answers to the questions we develop on texts, as we try out ahead of time the exercises we plan to use in the group, as we pray beforehand, as we lead the centering or listen to the discussion or do the final exercise alongside others, we are already in the process of being fed. But we can scarcely leave it at that. We also may need to be monitoring our dreams, keeping a journal in which we reflect on our own inner reality and its intersections with outer events, engaging in some form of meditation, and stimulating our minds with new sources of insight and reflection. Workshops, retreats, and psychotherapy might help. Spiritual discipline can be a discouraging business. Our activist, verbal left hemispheres quickly tire of the silence and waiting necessary to let the most subtle elements of the self emerge into awareness. But even if we are unable to adhere to a total regimen, we must find ways of working with those aspects of the self which most stand in the way of creative and nonegocentric leadership.

The Leader's Presuppositions

We need to be changed. But that is not all. Our very way of regarding knowledge must be changed as well. For the presuppositions underlying the way we have been taught to regard "knowing" are antithetical to the open-ended inquiry that characterizes the questioning approach.

The ideal of knowledge which has dominated biblical exegesis, seminary curricula, and the Western educational system as a whole, down to the lowest grades, is that of the encyclopedia. An educated person is one who "knows" as much of the contents of the encyclopedia (or of the total fund of data) as possible. Education consists then largely of unzipping empty heads, filling them full, and zipping them up again—and hoping that not everything leaks out! Almost no interest is shown in teaching others actually how to *think*. This view of knowledge can be described as a truncated pyramid:

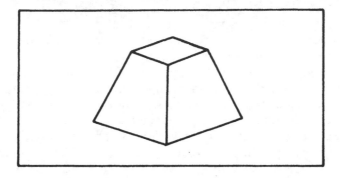

What is already known makes up the base of this pyramid, and the goal of research is to complete the pyramid by reducing the unknown to the vanishing point. Questions are not understood as probes into the infinite, but as way stations to right answers, which continually push back the frontiers of the uncomprehended.

This is a model of control, premised on a profound anxiety in the face of the unknown. It places the human agent of learning outside what is being examined, as a detached and uninvolved observer. Consequently the knower tends, in the very act of knowing, to become alienated from that which is known.

Like the God of classical philosophy, we stand outside the system, analyzing, manipulating, controlling it. No matter how beautiful, complex, or majestic that which is being examined, the human examiner, by virtue of his powers of description, is deemed superior to it. He is external to it, godlike; he dominates it, as subject over object. Even when he examines himself, he stands outside himself, treating himself as an object and alienating himself from himself.

This left-brain "paradigm" or model of knowledge was ideal for subjugating nature. It provided a kind of distance from the stream of existence which enabled us to examine it with objectivity and detachment. It stripped nature of both gods and devils, rendering it benign and approachable. Now, at the end of the twentieth century, however, nature is exacting from us a penalty beyond our bearing for the way we have raped and pillaged it, and our own natures cry out for some sense of meaningful belonging to the whole.

The new "paradigm" of knowledge now emerging in all fields of thought calls for inverting this pyramid, with the recognition that knowledge opens out into the unknown infinitely, mysteriously, wondrously.

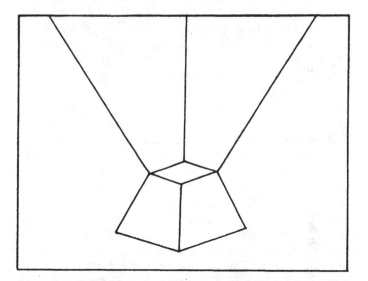

The optical illusion (do you see it?) aptly illustrates the issue, for these two paradigms of knowledge are incommensurable. Either you see the one, or you see the other. You cannot see them both at the same time. In fact, however, the eye can rest with neither but oscillates between the two. It is an especially appropriate model of the new way of perceiving reality, for we may need to pass through the lower to reach the upper, to memorize and internalize before we can think, to learn (and always to continue to try to learn more) about reality. But there comes a time when we pass from "knowing about" reality, to *knowing* it—a point when we go "through the looking glass," "through the eye of the needle," "through the wardrobe door," in order to enter another dimension where the more we know, the more we know we do not know; where everything we learn reveals how much more there is to learn; where we live the question through a score of right answers, all of which we make our own, without ever exhausting the generative power of the question; where awe and wonder are the only adequate response to the mystery that continually reveals itself as greater still. Instead of competitively struggling to scramble to the top of the pyramid first, we can now assist one another in finding truths whose discovery gives no one a personal advantage over others. The new, as it were, takes up the old into itself, builds upon the old, but is not simply something "added on." To enter the new, as Jesus made clear, we have to die to that which is *merely* the old. We have to lose our lives to find them.

Bible study for human transformation cannot then be regarded as just a new technique. It depends on a whole new paradigm: new presuppositions, new values, new methods, new beliefs, a new view of knowledge, a person being made new. One who is locked in the old paradigm, who really believes that the "one right answer" is more important than the question, will treat people as receptacles for information rather than organisms equipped to discover truth. Such a person will inevitably manipulate others through the questions in order to force them to arrive at foreordained conclusions, or else he will find himself continually reverting to the lecturing mode. It is not easy to find the key to that invisible door, though there be a thousand paths to it. . . .

The Leader's Preparation

Background Information. An approach as demanding as this can scarcely be undertaken without serious study of biblical resources. The more one knows about the text and the period under study, the more penetrating will be the questions one shapes, and the more able one will be to field questions that arise within the group. Knowing a great deal can also be a hazard, of course. We may think we know what the text is all about because someone else said so, instead of coming to it fresh and openly. Or we may be tempted to a kind of cocky assurance that pretends to know more than it does. There is no disgrace—in fact, considerable grace—in being able to say, "I don't know." Nevertheless, the serious leader will want continually to deepen her understanding of the world out of which these texts came. To that end, there is a brief bibliography at the end of the book, limited to the Synoptic Gospels, of essential reference works invaluable in all preparation, and other titles related to this approach.

Preparation for the Session. It should be clear by now that one can scarcely walk into a session unprepared and expect the gates of profundity to fall off their hinges. I recall a training session where one leader, confident of his general skill at group leadership and his knowledge of the Bible, decided to "wing it" without consulting any commentaries. The passage he had chosen was the parable of the strong man in Mark 3:27 par., whose immediate context (the sayings about Jesus' being possessed by Beelzebul and the sin against the Holy Spirit) provides as many enigmas as any passage in Scripture. Not far into the session it became clear that he had assumed without reflection (contrary to the whole history of interpretation and everyone's perception in the room) that the "strong man" referred to Jesus instead of Satan. There was nothing to do but stop, since all of his questions were premised on an assumption that he was not prepared to defend and of whose problematic nature he was not even aware.

This does not mean that only seminary-trained pastors or highly intelligent laity are capable of leading in this mode. Scripture was, after all, written for the whole people of God, and is therefore usually intelligible to any of us willing to take the time to learn something about it. Where it is most unintelligible is usually where customs or thought-forms are most different from ours, and here commentaries may prove invaluable.

Feedback. We all need help in improving, especially in an approach such as this where we learn best by trial and error. It might prove useful then to structure into the group process times for general feedback on how the group is going. You might also ask the more perceptive members privately for their constructive criticisms. This is not always easy for them to give, however. If they perceive you as needing reassurance, or if they have put you on a pedestal (as a clergy person, for example), or if they are afraid you will equate a negative reaction with a personal attack, they will do little more than tell you what they think you want to hear. Or they may not be clear enough about your objectives or the process to know how to criticize what you have done.

Even when you do get strong negative feedback, you have to listen carefully with the third ear to discern whether it comes from a central place in the self or is egocentrically motivated. Does it come, for example, from resistance to being "forced" to face buried terrors or unforgiven wounds that they would rather avoid? Are members of the group inappropriately comparing what you are attempting with other models (sensitivity training labs, encounter groups, charismatic prayer fellowships, Serendipity, Relational Bible Study, and so on) without first assessing this approach on its own merits? Are they operating under the old paradigm of knowledge, and expecting more factual information? Is their criticism a mask for a negative emotion which they have not owned, such as resistance to submitting to your authority as leader? It is not always easy to know which criticisms deserve attention. If we are very nervous and insecure (as most of us invariably are in trying something new) we need to get some distance on the session, become as centered as we can, and hold each criticism up against what the Holy Spirit was actually doing within the group process.

Often something wonderful happens *because* of a very sloppy and indefensible piece of leadership, and someone may see only the sloppiness and not the wonder. I once expressed sharp anger at one person in the group. On most other occasions I would have been disgusted with myself; this time, however, the anger seemed to me to come from a very centered place in me. I felt that it had an objective quality, and was spoken out of a very fierce love. He and I became closer because of it. When I later received a letter from someone else in the group castigating me for my unprofessional and unchristian outburst, I simply had to say: "Maybe she's right, God only knows. But I don't believe she's right, in my own deep self." If we are prepared thus to "sin" boldly, but trust in God's grace more boldly still, we can offer the Spirit a far broader range of strings to strike in bringing about what is needed in the transformation of others. And when what comes out is a clear discord, we can also learn from that and go on, confident that the Spirit can use even such imperfect instruments as we.

Chapter 6

Developing and Using Questions

Preparing Your Own Questions

The heart of this approach, of course, is the questions one asks. The Guild for Psychological Studies is preparing a set on the Synoptic Gospels. And I have provided some in the last chapter of this book. In developing your own questions, however, it is absolutely essential to make up a preliminary set *before* looking at anyone else's questions. Nor would I recommend consulting any secondary "authorities," such as commentaries, until you have discovered what your own questions are. We have been trained for so long to regard the scholars as experts that we can scarcely resist deferring to their expertise. Once we have read what they have to say, the text will tell us only what they have told us that it says. And since the historical critical method is incapable of handling questions of truth, these resources, invaluable as they are, often do not even address the most fundamental issues in the texts.

It is all the more important then that you first read through the biblical text several times, and then make out a preliminary set of questions, asking everything that pops into mind—*before* consulting any reference works of any kind—and also before referring to anyone else's questions (mine included). It is especially valuable to ask questions for which we have no right to expect an answer, at least in any definitive sense. These sometimes open windows into the deepest mystery of what is being communicated—questions like, What is implied about the nature of God here? What kind of consciousness was required for Jesus to say this? Then, having made our provisional list of questions, we turn, gratefully and with muted anticipation, to the secondary sources. Now we know what we are looking for. We go with our own sense of authority. In these books we may discover that some of our hunches were all wrong. We may hit on new questions we hadn't seen, or refine our questions more precisely. Beyond all that, the critical resources give a dimension of depth to our background preparation, and enhance our confidence that our questions in fact do derive from the questions which originally brought the text into being.

The lazy-minded, harassed by busy schedules and long since having given up on the scholarly tools because they found them of so little help, may be tempted to rush into a group with a quickly prepared list of questions and no additional preparation. (Or they may be tempted to use questions developed by someone else without feeling their way into them for themselves.) Truly, as Jesus so laconically put it, "they have their reward": superficial discussion that seldom moves beyond what everyone knew before the session began.

Developing profound questions is the most crucial aspect, and most difficult part, of leadership in this mode. There is no way I know to teach others how to formulate good questions. It is best learned by exposure to the leadership of others more experienced. Often we fail to be aware of entire dimensions of meaning in a text. Our preunderstanding blinds us to other possible interpretations. Questions we have been trained not to ask never even rise to consciousness, so anxious are we to avoid heresy, or to avoid stirring up issues and feelings for which we have no present antidote.

There are, however, a few things that we can do to open ourselves to the widest possible range of meanings in the text. We can begin by consciously suspending our assurance that we know the answer. We can deliberately bring ourselves to look at the text from unaccustomed angles. We can try with all our powers to come to the text as supplicants with our hands outstretched, entreating it to speak to us in its own right. This attitude typifies the scientific mentality at its best, and is far and away the greatest contribution of the critical approach to the study of the Bible.

What kinds of questions are most important to ask? The critical questions are provided by the critical problems which the text presents: How do the several versions of a saying differ, and why? What are the customs that are presupposed in the narrative? How might the statement have been modified by the church in order to apply it to later crises and conflicts? "Critical" simply means concern to do justice to the *foreignness* of the passage: what it meant in its own context, what linguistic, literary, and historical information is essential for its understanding, what modifications it may have undergone in its pilgrimage to its present position in Scripture.

Likewise, questions relating to amplifying the text will largely be given by its very structure. In the example provided in chapter 3, the largest number of questions were aimed simply at uncovering the logic and meaning of the saying itself. (What is Jesus saying here about judging? What is the relationship between the log and the splinter? and so on.)

Sometimes a text will be best served by raising all the critical questions first, before proceeding to amplification. At other times the critical questions (and necessary critical information) can be unobtrusively woven into the general movement of amplification. An example of the latter appeared in chapter 3 when the group was asked which best summed up the point of the whole paragraph on loving enemies—Matthew's "Be perfect" or Luke's "Be merciful"? In that case someone in the group asked for further critical information, which the leader then was able to supply (the Aramaic and Greek terms for "perfect"). Whenever you supply information this way, however, try to be brief, and to conclude with a question, such as, "What further light might that shed on the meaning of the passage?" Avoid parading your learning or giving mini-lectures. You will appear to be giving the final answer rather than supplying aids to understanding, and will throttle the initiative of the others in the group. The leader is called upon to sacrifice much of what she or he has learned, in order to facilitate the discovery of even a fraction of it by others. Those of us who are "rich" in information and training are invited to become "poor" that we might make others rich. It requires real discernment (and a great deal of practice) to distinguish essential data from unessential. Most of us will, at the beginning, err on the side of giving too much information.

Perhaps we will be guided best if we keep in mind that the goal is not educating biblically illiterate Christians, but rather aiding them to discover life-changing truths in the text. *The payoff is not information but transformation.* To that end, make your questions as simple and clear as possible. Never ask several things in one question. Avoid two- and three-part questions. Never ask a question that can be answered yes or no. Formulate broad questions that do not set people up for a specific answer. Try to find ways to enable people to become fully involved in the material, intellectually and personally, bringing both thought and feeling to the exploration of the meaning of the text and its possible implications for themselves. A good test of your questions is to go through your final set, trying to give at least two good answers to each question yourself. That will ensure that you have weeded out leading or rhetorical questions (questions that imply a specific answer).

People are sometimes confused when we move from asking critical questions (for which there sometimes *are* right answers—such as "Who were the Samaritans?") to the more fundamental questions, for which there are many right answers, no one of which is solely correct. I have found no way to prevent this confusion. Generally people seem to sense the difference, but you might simply note it in your introduction.

One of the most fruitful lines of questioning lies in exploring the meaning of images and symbols. Modern thought is so abstract that most people are initially incapable of perceiving symbols as anything more than picturesque turns of phrase or primitive thought-forms. They scarcely even sense that powerful symbols are like hydrogen atoms on the verge of fusion. To trigger them, to permit them to explode into meaning, requires our feeling into the image. Thought, already abstracted, cannot do it. Try to get people to *see* the image and to describe what they see. When they relapse into abstract statements, recall them once more to visual or tactile statements, until the group has a felt sense of the symbol. Then you can proceed to ask about its meaning.

The baptism of Jesus provides a rich concentration of especially potent symbols (Mark 1:9-11 par.). Instead of informing the group that the phrase "the heavens opened" is a commonplace of apocalyptic symbolism, referring to the moment of revelation, ask them to feel into the image. "What is about to happen? The words in Mark are literally, 'the heavens were ripped open.' Coming on the heels of John's preaching, what does that way of phrasing it lead you to expect out of heaven? What does come? Why this sudden dovish reversal?" The same process of feeling into the symbolism could be repeated for the dove, water, and the act of baptism. When we take such symbols seriously at their profound, archetypal level, they are capable of revealing depths of meaning far beyond anything we can grasp by our more usual, left-brain mode of thinking.

Many of the most penetrating questions are not self-evident in the passage, but have to be probed for as the essential presuppositions underlying it. The most illuminating (and most difficult), I believe, are those which relate to the nature of the God-image implied by the text and its relationship to the actual, functioning God-image within us. Allied to that is the question, How did Jesus himself personally relate to God, as this is revealed in what he taught? Many people would avoid these questions, having long since settled them for themselves. Others would regard them as being illegitimate, given the nature of the text's long series of modifications at the hands of the church. But the questions are legitimate nonetheless, even if we can never be certain when Jesus is speaking and when it is the church. For Jesus' understanding of existence *is* preserved in the Gospels, as Bultmann correctly perceived, and the patterns of the church's alterations of Jesus' seminal thought are clear enough in their broad outlines.

In any case, our goal is not an absolute historical certainty. That mentality merely substituted historical inerrancy for literal inerrancy as a guarantor of truth. For my own part, I think that the notion that something had to happen in order to be true is just as preposterous as the idea that the Bible has to have been dictated by the Holy Spirit, word for word, in order to be true. What we seek in this approach is not an authoritative truth to which one is bound to consent, but an encounter with understandings of God and of human life which can call our own lives into question, open new vistas of possibility, and empower us to be transformed.

It is not all that helpful, then, to go through the text simply asking what I would call "surface" questions. Take Mark 9:38-40 par., for example:

Mark 9:38-40	Luke 9:49-50
38 John said to him, "Teacher, we saw a man casting out demons in your name, and we forbade him, because he was not following us."	49 John answered, "Master, we saw a man casting out demons in your name, and we forbade him, because he does not follow with us."
39But Jesus said, "Do not forbid him; for no one who does a mighty work in my name will be able soon after to speak evil of me.	50But Jesus said to him, "Do not forbid him;
40For he that is not against us is for us.	for he that is not against you is for you."

One could easily just ask the obvious: "Who is this 'John'? Why doesn't he want someone outside the group to exorcise in Jesus' name? Why does Jesus not forbid such practice? What does he mean by verse 40?" But there are far deeper issues here. "To what degree does this passage reflect the experience of the early church? Why does John say, 'Following us,' not 'you'? Compare Numbers 11:24-30. What kind of faith does the exorcist have? Is this faith or magic? Did Jesus cast out demons in his own name? How did he? What would have happened if the exorcist had dropped the name of Jesus? Could he still have exorcised? What is he projecting onto Jesus? What would it mean for us to be in touch with the same power Jesus was in touch with here? How do we in the church get caught in the disciples' reaction today? Who are the 'strange exorcists' who irritate us most?" Now several concrete issues of current urgency have been joined: What is the nature of faith? How does it operate? What is Jesus' role in evoking faith? What is Jesus' relationship to the power of God? What might ours be? And what are our attitudes toward faith healers and exorcists, charismatics and psychics today? None of these last issues need to be explicitly raised, since they are implicit in the questions and in the text. But many people will not be aware of their presence in the text unless your questions open up these dimensions of possible reflection for them.

It cannot be stressed enough, however, that we are not just intent on "milking" the text for some subjective meaning. We are asking, first of all, what the passage itself seems to be saying about these weighty and mysterious themes. Then we can apply the text to ourselves, comparing our situation with that in the text, internalizing some aspects of the account, exploring its symbolic meaning, or encountering its ethical challenge. It is usually best to treat the original meaning of the text *before* we ask its meaning now. If this order is not maintained, the group may risk "psychologizing" the passage and will miss a chance for hearing the text say something quite *different* from what we had expected, or even something we would rather *not* hear. (See Appendix 3, "On Psychologizing.") But even this is not a rule that may not be broken.

I have found it helpful, once I have formulated my critical and amplification questions, and before attempting to formulate an application exercise that faces us with the text's possible relevance for today, to ask myself: Now, in the light of all these lesser questions, what is the *big* question that is handled in this text? Many texts appear to have a single "big question." The "Confession of Peter" (Mark 8:27-33 par.), for example, seems to ask of us, "Who is this Jesus, really?" The Temptation Narrative (Matt. 4:1-11; Mark 1:12-13; Luke 4:1-13), on the other hand, is so rich a narrative that one could conceivably identify a whole series of "big questions": What is the role of temptation/testing in spiritual growth? What is the role of Satan in choice? What is the relation of the Holy Spirit and Satan? How do we discern the will of God? How did Jesus relate to the messianic images alive in Judaism? All these issues will probably be touched on in the study, but the leader will have to choose a point to focus on, perhaps depending on the theme which is currently pursued in the study series.

By identifying the big question, it is possible then to

develop an application exercise which is congruous with the text. If you are working with the Temptation Narrative and are focusing on the role of Satan in it, you might conclude by having people take a large sheet of paper, turn it so the length is sideways, and draw a line down the middle. In the left panel, invite them to draw a picture (I much prefer oil pastels to crayons) of the Satan they grew up with, whether they believed in this Satan or not. Then in the right panel, draw the understanding of Satan that has emerged from this story, and share.

Or if you are focusing on the role of temptation in spiritual growth, you might have the group subdivide into threesomes and each share for a few moments which of these three temptations is most characteristic of them at this stage of their lives. (These are all temptations to misuse power, not carnal temptations, so people should not find it difficult to share. You might add a fourth temptation, unfortunately all too characteristic of many Christians: the avoidance of power altogether for fear of misusing it.)

Preparing for the Group

Once you have developed a finished set of questions, they should then be ordered in a sequence that follows as much as possible the actual sequence of the text. Generally one does well to avoid being too clever in one's questions, leaping around from the beginning of the text to the end and back again. People are able to trust your questions better if you go through verse by verse, and let the structure of the text itself provide the structure of the dialogue. Otherwise they may suspect that you have a special agenda that you have imported into the text, and will tend to balk at your leadership.

Next, become thoroughly familiar with your questions, so that as other questions arise from the group they can also be integrated into the given sequence of questions without abandoning the basic structure. The leader should never jettison the line of questioning entirely, no matter what questions are introduced, if in fact the original questions faithfully uncover the inner dynamic of the text. Spontaneity is encouraged within a clear order—and this not through any rigidity on the leader's part, but because the goal is faithfully to serve the understanding of the text, and in most cases only the leader has devoted the time and study necessary to represent its interests adequately.

Before the session begins, be sure that the chairs are arranged in a close circle. One reason is aesthetic: it is pleasing to the eye. Another is practical: people can hear better. When someone wants to sit outside the circle, he or she is making a statement to the group—"I don't want to buy into this process fully," or "I feel inadequate to participate," or "If I can't lead I will observe." I simply will not start until each person comes all the way in, where everyone is equal with everyone else and can be seen and heard by all. Another reason is symbolic. The circle is a profound image of wholeness, of organic unity, of safety. The group becomes a living mandala, a sacred wheel representing "both the wholeness desired by each person present and also the container in which the work is carried on."[1]

In preparing, save the last hour or so to center down, praying over your questions (for trust in them and in the process) and for each person (if it is a group you know). Open yourself to the creative possibilities that can be effected by God's Spirit.

Having prepared as thoroughly as possible, say to yourself: "I know only a fraction of what this text is all about. I come to it with the group, as if for the first time, prepared to hear something I never knew." Try to adopt a "beginner's mind." As leaders, our needs are as great as anyone's in the group, and it is, after all, only the empty cup that can be filled. Come prepared to lead. Come also to be fed.

Chapter 7

Introducing Biblical Criticism

The Value of the Critical Approach

In a short series of Bible studies, historical critical issues can often be skirted, especially if the passages selected present few critical problems (such as certain of the parables). In a longer series, or in a group committed to serious study, some introduction to the problems of critical study is necessary, however, whether it be the "synoptic problem" (the question of the interrelation of the three Gospels which can be seen "alongside each other," or *syn-optically*), or the development of Old Testament traditions through centuries of accretions and editings. This work is called "criticism" (from the Greek *krisis*, "judgment") because it takes an analytical stance toward Scripture. It does not submit to the Bible as an unquestionable authority, but raises questions regarding its composition, date, authorship, and meaning. It seeks to recover the precise historical setting that gave it its original relevance. It prevents us from applying the text superficially to our own situation by demonstrating how very different, foreign, incommensurate, and nontransferable their situation may be in reference to ours.

If left there, of course (as in fact happens in much modern criticism), the text is simply alienated from us. Conservatives and fundamentalists rightly protest against "higher criticism" when it thus robs us of the Bible's capacity to speak meaningfully to our lives.

Despite this danger, however, biblical criticism can be an invaluable instrument in our emancipation from doctrines that stunt growth and muzzle Scripture. It can release us from the dogmas of biblical inerrancy and verbal inspiration, which impose an external authority residing in particular denominations and their theological custodians, the preachers. Criticism can free us to be honest about what we see in the text—for what we see (and may have been taught not to acknowledge to ourselves or to raise questions about) is in fact often *there*. Critical study permits us to ask every question that comes to mind, no matter how "heretical," "blasphemous," or "impious." It can help us see the various stages of development in a passage, how the passage has been altered in order to apply it to new situations, how it has been modified in order to water it down or to increase its rigor. And biblical criticism can enable us to distinguish Jesus' own self-understanding from that later developed by the church, thereby providing what Van Harvey called a second avenue of access to the transformative reality lived out by Jesus.[1]

I am not here calling for a return to the "liberal Jesus," whose ethical teachings about "the fatherhood of God and the brotherhood of man" formed the basis for the optimistic rationalism of nineteenth-century liberalism. I am speaking rather from the vantage point of depth psychology and the new understandings of myth developed by Jung, Ricoeur, and Eliade. The issue is recovering Jesus' own myth in distinction to the myth of Jesus. In short, biblical criticism can liberate the intellect to radical truthfulness, personal integrity, and rational responsibility. No genuine individuation is possible without such qualities. We can be grateful for the "acid bath" of critical reflection, even as we are aware of its profound limitations.

I have discussed these limitations at some length in *The Bible in Human Transformation*, but a brief recapitulation of its thesis might be of service here. For if biblical criticism is to achieve its goal, it must not be permitted to get "stuck," as it has of late, in an alienated past inaccessible to the scorching questions of today. Whenever criticism abandons the emancipatory intent with which it began, it becomes a stifling orthodoxy in its own right, swept along by the momentum of its own technical apparatus and indifferent to the life questions which gave birth to the texts themselves and to the scholars' original interest in studying them. Like the wealthy cargo of the merchant ships in Revelation 18, much biblical scholarship has become a feature of the decadence of the

West, a luxury good, largely unrelated to the struggles of real people for liberation, dignity, or a reason to live. This is a development that has moved apace in the last two decades, as biblical scholarship has increasingly been divorced from vital communities. Scholars increasingly look to the universities and to their own peers in the professional societies as their community of accountability. The questions they ask are not those on which human survival and development hinge, but those for which their technology can provide answers.

We have moved into a period of prolific publication of works read by fewer and fewer readers in enclaves peopled only by similar technicians, while the church and world stagger along their desperate course largely unaided by the guardians of the world's greatest treasure.

Nor can that treasure be made accessible by lectures on biblical criticism and history. People must be enabled to discover their own critical capacities, their own intellectual depth, and the right and ability to think for themselves. The critical material itself, then, is best presented when people can discover it for themselves. Otherwise we provide answers to questions people have never even asked.

This process of helping people stumble upon the critical problems themselves is especially valuable in fundamentalist circles, where a lecture on biblical criticism would have an effect comparable to spraying gasoline on a grass fire. Here is how one pastor, Ronald Allen, described in a letter the way he introduced biblical criticism to a Colorado parish:

> Most of the people were hard-line fundamentalists or extremely conservative, deeply committed to the church and "following Jesus." They invited me to lead them in a series of studies, which I did, using the material beginning with John the Baptist. Since they did not have *Gospel Parallels* I mimeographed parallel accounts for the ten or eleven sessions we had together. The first session, just looking at the sources, was electrifying. The best thing that happened that first night was that *they*, led by the questions, made their own rebuttal of the fundamentalist paradigm. Of course, the battle wasn't won that one night, but the fact that they made the discovery was later identified as a turning point.

Most of the laity, however, are not motivated enough to begin with critical study. In that case it may be better not to begin with an introduction to the synoptic problem (or any other critical survey). You might start instead with a series of passages of arresting depth, so that people immediately sense the urgency of the work for their lives. Then, as you bring in aspects of the critical material along the way, it will increasingly commend itself as helpful, and they will become more open to dealing with it. (Most often the people with whom I work are not so much offended by the critical introductory material as unable to grasp its immediate relevance, and want to get on to more personally engaging questions.)

Introducing the Synoptic Problem

For those groups ready for such inquiry, here is one way of helping them discover for themselves the nature of the critical task.

1. Read carefully the three columns of Matthew, Mark, and Luke in *Records* (¶ 17-18) or *Parallels* (¶ 1-6)—Matt. 3:1-17; Mark 1:1-11; Luke 3:1-22. Note especially their similarities and differences. (Allow time for this.) What did you discover? (Photocopy the texts if necessary. Have people share, going through one section at a time. If they fail to notice significant data, don't tell them; ask a question: "How about vs. 2 in Mark? Where is that quotation actually from?")

2. Why do Matthew and Luke not have Mark's beginning (1:1)? With what do they begin? By starting this way, Mark gives the impression that Jesus became Son of God when? Matthew and Luke suggest when?

3. Matthew and Luke don't have Mark 1:2. Why? Where is the quote here really from?

4. Luke quotes more of the Isaiah passage than the others. Why? How does vs. 6 serve the purposes for which Luke writes?

5. Apparently Matthew believed that forgiveness of sins is brought about only through the cross of Jesus

(Matt. 26:28). What light might this shed on the way he characterizes John's preaching in vs. 2?

6. Note the high degree of similarity between Matt. 3:7-10 and Luke 3:7-9. How would you account for the difference in the audience addressed? Mark doesn't have this material. Why?

7. Only Luke has 3:10-14. Where might he have gotten it?

8. In Mark 1:7-8, Matthew and Luke differ together how? What might that suggest about their sources for this section?

9. Matt. 3:12 and Luke 3:17 are again missing in Mark. How would you account for that?

10. Look at Luke 3:19-20. Apparently there was a group of John's followers who lasted well into the second century, declaring John to be the Messiah, not Jesus. John's superiority was evident in the fact that he baptized Jesus. How might Luke be countering that kind of argument here? Where do Matthew and Mark place this section? Is Jesus baptized by John or not, according to Luke?

11. In Matt. 3:14-15, Matthew might be dealing with John's continuing disciples how? And the church believed Jesus to be sinless (see the footnote reference to the *Gospel according to the Hebrews*); how might Matthew be dealing with that problem? What do you think is the source of these verses? Do you think they are historical?

12. Which do you think is earlier, the Holy Spirit "like a dove," or "in bodily form, as a dove"? Which is earlier, "This is" or "Thou art"?

13. The Greek for "opened" in Mark is "was rent" or "torn asunder"; Matthew and Luke have the word "to open." Which strikes you as more original to the account?

14. Which account seems to you to be earliest? List the evidence. Which seems to have the most developed view of Jesus as the Christ?

15. On the basis of what you have seen here, how would you suppose these three Gospels are related? Do you

think they were written independently of one another? How would you account for the agreements between them, not only in wording but in the order in which the material appears? What sources would you guess went to make up the sections we looked at?

16. Look over the three Gospels as a whole; where do they *stop* being parallel? Where do they *start* being parallel? Virtually all of Mark is found in Matthew and Luke (610 out of 661 verses). Mark's order is always in agreement with either Matthew's or Luke's, and where one is not in agreement the other always is. This agreement of Matthew and Luke with each other begins where Mark begins and ends where Mark ends. What does that suggest about their relationship? When Matthew, Mark, and Luke all agree, we're really only talking about how many sources?

17. We also saw that occasionally Matthew and Luke have common material not shared by Mark. This has often been called "Q" (from the German *Quelle,* or "source"). Matthew and Luke appear to have drawn on this hypothetical source independently. It apparently was a written document and not just oral tradition, since Matthew and Luke both use it in approximately the same order, despite the fact that they use it in different contexts. Apparently they used it independent of each other, rather than the one copying it from the other, since sometimes Matthew's version of a saying, and sometimes Luke's, seems to be more original. If one were copying from the other, we would expect the earlier one to be more consistently original.

All this is hypothetical, of course, and some scholars have proposed quite different solutions. (For a review, see W. G. Kümmel, *Introduction to the New Testament,* rev. ed., chapter 5.)

When we add additional special oral traditions known only to Matthew ("M") and to Luke ("L"), the hypothesized sketch of the relationship between the three Gospels is as follows:

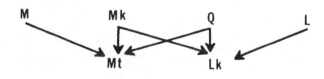

A full introduction could then go on to help the group discover for itself the extent of the "Q" material, learn to identify conflation, editorial additions, Luke's special passion source, and so forth.

This kind of digging will prove fascinating and liberating for some, frustrating or threatening or boring for others. But it is invaluable in the long-term struggle for the liberation of the intellect and the capacity of individuals to make their own choices. In terms of the functions of the brain, critical reflection enables the left hemisphere to gain analytical distance from the received tradition. From a distance we can see certain things for the first time. We are able to reassess their meaning and authority. And on the basis of our analytical reflections we can then (with the aid of the right hemisphere) discover new possibilities of truth and meaning unknown to us before. Critical reflection is not creativity, but it is its indispensable ground. The truth that transforms is finally not possible without it, whether we learn to question the tradition from teachers or from the sheer desperateness of our lives.

Chapter 8

Engaging the Other Side of the Brain

Insights are not just fresh ideas. They are the flicker of new life-possibilities emerging into our sight. A moment's delay in apprehending them, and the glimmer fades—they are lost. Insights are so evanescent precisely because they are foreign to the received wisdom by which we habitually operate. The transformation they promise also promises disruption of the known ways. We have a stake in receiving them; we have a stake in keeping them away. The point of the application exercises is to clear a space for insights to come; to provide the means by which they can be objectified, made tangible, visible, public; and to allow us to choose to incorporate them, with group support, into our lives.

It is a curious fact that the most relevatory insights have most often come to people, not during the more intellectual discussion of the text, but in the application exercises, when they were painting, dialoguing, or working with clay. This is not surprising, once we overcome the bias of intellectualism. As brain researcher Paul MacLean puts it, "Subjectively, something doesn't exist unless it's tied up with an emotion."[1] Insights are not simply left-brain phenomena. They are born of the confluence of thought and feeling, the synthesis of left and right hemispheres of the brain. Critical study and amplification of the text allows us to see it in a new way, to feel into the dynamic of the narrative, the characters, or the saying. An inchoate hunch is engendered, wordless, wanting to be born. If we stop with the exegesis, it aborts, unformed. People go away entertained, with new ideas, with increased knowledge of the Scriptures—and with the dead fetus of an insight that has miscarried because we cut off the process too soon.

Perhaps the most frequent failing among those who try this approach is their omission of any exercise that could evoke more than just an intellectual response. When pressed, they admit that they really felt *relieved* about omitting them: they were anxious about doing the exercises, feared the resistance of the group (or certain members), and may have even, to some degree, unconsciously maneuvered things so they would not have time to do them.

I understand that perfectly. I have done the same. Sometimes I have judged the group's potential resistance altogether wrongly, however. Once I almost dropped the exercise because I feared that shouting the Lord's Prayer would offend some of the more conservative members of the group; after we did it, it was several of those people who were most moved. Another time I thought twice about assigning painting to a group of mostly retired persons. I plunged ahead anyway. Few of them got very involved, it turned out, but two younger members of the group plowed up some terribly painful unforgiven terrain. They had the courage to share it with these older persons who represented their worst fears of rejection by the community, and when these people met their fears with understanding love, the miracle of new life occurred. Once I almost thought better than to ask a group which had not shown much creativity to write their own parables. I went ahead with it, however, and was astonished at the extraordinary parables of an eighty-three-year-old woman who had never tried anything like it before. This was a turning point in her life. She had never tapped her creative powers before. She came alive, as she puts it, for the first time; she is now giving book reviews on works like *Zen and the Art of Motorcycle Maintenance,* is learning Spanish, studying biblical history, and generally proving that transformation can happen to anyone at any age.

Perhaps an irascible member of the group will snort at the assigned exercise and refuse to do it. Challenge him to try it as an experiment. *Do not make it optional.* People have contracted for the whole process, and are free to decide *afterward* whether it was worthwhile. Often, those who titter through the task, or do it peremptorily, or refuse to do it at all, will be ashamed when they see how profoundly moved others have been, will secretly wish they had taken it more seriously, and the next time (when you are anxiously expecting their continued resistance and being tempted to omit the exercise) *they* will be the ones most eager to try it. (For this reason it is important to insist that these exercises be carried out in complete silence.)

So it is easier in the long run if you simply fix it in your mind that the group is going to do the exercise, plan the discussion so as to ensure adequate time for it, and then treat the resistance you encounter as good-naturedly as you can. *Irrational resistance should never be honored as a serious objection to your own conscientious preparation.* If your activity misses the mark, let that come out in feedback at the end.

This resistance is grounded in the very structure of the brain. The left hemisphere, so used to being in control, is immediately threatened by many of these exercises, with their stress on right-brain activity. The left brain likes to be boss, as Betty Edwards put it, and prefers not to relinquish tasks to its "inferior" partner unless it really dislikes the job or is overwhelmed by its complexity.[2] What we need then are exercises which at least can partially block the left brain by presenting it with activities which it either cannot or will not do, thus allowing the right brain to get engaged with the text in ways that will permit it to express itself and be affected by what it encounters in the text.

As a way of fostering your own creativity and imaginative innovation in the development of application exercises, here is a partial listing of some that have proved useful. Most of them come originally from the Guild for Psychological Studies. None of these should be considered normative or be woodenly adopted. Every exercise must be integral to the text and serve the major thrust that your line of questions has uncovered. Far better to do no exercise at all than one pulled in from outside the range of the text's concerns. People may enjoy the activity but be at a total loss to relate it to anything that has gone before. (I often am unable to develop an appropriate exercise. When that happens, I at least try to zero in hard on a question that engages the text with our own lives today.)

These activities are capable of striking deep archetypal

chords in the unconscious, chords already set vibrating by discussion of the text but not fully activated. If we wish to receive not just new ideas, but new ways of being and doing, this deep repository of memory, meaning, and commitment must be activated. Precisely because these activities can move at such a depth, however, it is important also to be aware of their hazards. Some understanding of how the unconscious functions can be of immeasurable benefit here, for while these exercises "work" whether we understand them or not, we will be far better equipped to develop and administer them if we have a practical knowledge of depth psychology, specifically the psychology of Carl Jung. And the more we know about the inner workings of our own psyches, the better positioned we will be to help others.

These exercises are intended to have a powerful impact. Nevertheless I believe they are generally safe when used sensibly and in the context of an explicit commitment to the religious journey. My experience has been that people will not go deeper than the trust and support level of the group justifies. If someone touches something so deep that he or she is frightened by it, there is always professional help nearby. And the difficulty was obviously already there anyway. In leading hundreds of groups I have only had one experience of a person going beyond her capacity to cope, and that was due to my failure to "de-role" a role-play situation. This is essentially a gentle approach. It does not manipulate or force, but rather establishes permissions that enable people to face what they have so long avoided. And if they choose to continue to avoid, they are free to do so. As a leader you may at first fear going too far. You will probably discover that your own resistance and that of the group prevents you from going far enough.

If you have never before tried the exercises you plan to do with the group, you will be well advised to try them out for yourself before leading your group. Having already experienced the impact of the exercise yourself, you will not be caught completely off guard by the responses of others. It is generally a good practice to bring people back together after each activity to share their experiences and insights. Such sharing further secures the insight by articulating it, and provides closure to the experience. And as leader, it is usually a good idea to participate in the exercise with the group.

One general word of caution: avoid exercises that involve identifying with Jesus. So much of the time readers of the New Testament *have* identified with him, owing to the natural tendency to project onto and identify with the hero in a story. The result is a kind of messianic inflation. If our goal is transformation, we are better served by consciously identifying with those persons in a story who need healing, help, and forgiveness, and seeking to *relate to* (rather than identify with) the healing, helping, forgiving reality which was alive in Jesus—and can be alive in us as well.

The following are then a sample of things you might do.

Paint Pictures. Any medium that people can use is fine. Sometimes a very quick picture done in five or ten minutes is enough to evoke a feeling response to the material, with people showing and perhaps also sharing what they have done. At other times an extended period should be allowed so that people can move more meditatively into the meaning of the passage for them. It is usually a richer experience, however, when they have a chance to share, either in the group or in smaller subgroups. Always be clear whether they are to portray the objective scene (such as the baptism, the temptation, or the crucifixion of Jesus), or their subjective, personal reaction to it. As an example of the latter, I conclude a discussion of the parable of the compassionate Samaritan (Luke 10:29-37) by asking people to identify with the wounded person in the story and to say what is the wounded part in them. After several responses, I suggest that everyone get art materials, which I have provided, and paint the wounded person or part in them, urging them to plunge beneath the superficial complaints to the basic or core life-wound: parental rejection, death of a parent or sibling or child, childhood traumas, divorce, whatever has not only hurt but continues to have aftereffects on us. After fifteen to twenty minutes, either have all reassemble and share what they wish about what they have drawn, or break into smaller groups if time is limited or the group is large. (It generally takes an hour for twenty people to share.) It is a good idea to discourage comments on the pictures by others. They may draw the person out more than she or he wishes, or people may fall into analyzing the picture, or complimenting the picture, or "rescuing" those touched by deep emotion. The goal, after all, is not group therapy, or competition to see who is the best artist, but simply self-expression leading to insight. It may even be advisable to reassure people at the beginning of the exercise that we have absolutely no interest in how artistic their pictures are, only how authentic. The "wound" many of us bear is precisely in our artistic capacities, which were ridiculed somewhere back in our early schooling, causing us to abandon them altogether. This exercise can not only lead to insight, then, but also begin the process of recovering lost capacities that are essential to our full selfhood.

Write Dialogues. Here is one way to introduce written dialogue with the "woman with the ointment" of Luke 7:36-50.

In order that we might get as deeply in touch with this woman in us as possible, I'd like to suggest that you write a dialogue between yourself and this woman as an inner aspect of yourself. We're not talking about the woman two thousand years ago. Don't ask her what Jesus was like, how she felt, and so on. Ask her to tell you about yourself, about how you have treated her, but also about the new life that she has found through Jesus. Talk to the woman in you, the woman whom this story has, as it were, put inside you. This woman is especially helpful as an inner wisdom guide because she not only knows what it means to be a sinner and a deviant who misuses her own sexual nature, but she has also experienced the inrush of forgiveness and love and is capable of boundless abandon to the Giver of life. As such she can tell us about that part of ourselves which we have rejected or repressed, or which has been declared deviant by us or by society. Don't try to control her voice. Let her say whatever she chooses. I start out by writing in the margin, "Me:" and I address her, possibly ask her a question; and then I put in the margin, "Woman:" and let her answer me however she wants. Try to give her complete freedom and autonomy to speak. You may feel that it's impossible, that you are talking to yourself. Try to silence that inner doubt and just let it flow. Let her say anything she wants to say, and let it come from anywhere that it wants to come from in yourself, and reflect on it only when you're finished. *We will not share the dialogues,* so feel free to let anything come out that wants to.

(At the end of twenty minutes or so, you can break them up into groups of four to six to share, not their dialogues, but any insights that they receive which they feel comfortable sharing, or simply whether the *process* was helpful or not. Or, if the experience is too private, you might forgo sharing and simply end with a prayer.)

It is essential that in writing dialogues our own egos always be involved, so that we do not identify our whole selves with the partial aspects of them with which we are dialoguing. If you are working with Jacob wrestling (Gen. 32:22-32), for example, you might write the dialogue between yourself ("me") and "Jacob" as an inner aspect of yourself. Perhaps you want also to engage Jacob's dark opponent in dialogue, so as to find that aspect in you (the adversary that can bless). Open the dialogue up then as a trialogue. But maintain the presence of your own ego, which alone can take responsibility for these many "selves" within us and work for their integration into a single whole. Besides, unless the conscious ego is involved, there is the danger of being inundated by autonomous psychic contents.[3]

Earlier I stressed the importance of not identifying with, but rather relating to, the redemptive figures in the Bible. Dialoguing can be an invaluable means of furthering that relatedness. What a shock it is—and what a gift—to write a dialogue with God, or the Holy Spirit, or the Son of man, or Jesus, and find ourselves being answered from beyond, spoken to out of the very depth of that reality which knows us better than we know ourselves. I cannot commend a better avenue for spiritual growth.

Dialogues done thus are among the safest, most consistently revelatory exercises one can do. In order to have real impact, however, the dialogue must be with a figure capable of evoking something deep in us. And many people have difficulty with their first attempt at dialogue. Keep trying though, because on the second or third effort remarkable things may happen, even to those who got nowhere the first time. This may require a courageous and dogged persistence on your part as leader, but you will find that the insights that come to people are staggering in their truth and impact.

Mime. The value of mime is that, unlike role playing, *each* person can identify with *all* the characters in turn. This prevents overidentification with a single character and allows us to recognize the external polarities that divide people as polarities in ourselves. In working through the overfamiliar parable of the compassionate Samaritan (Luke 10:29-37), for example, miming each character in turn can be a profoundly moving new point of entry into the story. This can be done by having everyone deployed with as much space as possible, yet within hearing range of the leader. First everyone acts out the role of the priest, walking along, discovering the wounded man, reacting, going on down the road. When all have come to a stop, the leader then announces that we are all now the Levite, then the wounded person, and finally the Samaritan. After the group reassembles, have them share how they felt in each role.

If there is inadequate space, or the group seems too inhibited to do the mime, you might instead ask them to remain seated in the circle with their eyes closed and *imagine* being each character in turn: "You are a priest, going down the Jericho road from Jerusalem, and as you come around a bend in a rocky defile you suddenly come upon a man, stripped, beaten, bloody, by the side of the road. And you feel how? (Ask them to speak out single words or phrases.) And as you pass by you feel how? Now be the Levite . . . the wounded person . . . the Samaritan. . . ." The point of either method is to get into a *feeling* relationship with the characters, in order to understand why the Samaritan could have compassion and the others could not.

Or we could mime the parable of the prodigal son (Luke 15:11-32) (really the prodigal father), so as to identify the aspects of us that are like the younger son and the elder brother. And by miming the father we can also become aware that there is that in us which is capable of reconciling them both. As we learn to see this polarity in ourselves, self-righteousness and us/them thinking become increasingly difficult, and we learn to love lost or rejected parts of ourselves—and others.

Or we could each mime the way the woman with the ointment (Luke 7:36-50) felt, first as she stood outside the door, then as she was at Jesus' feet, and finally as she hears him declare her sins forgiven. This could even serve as a lead-in to the written dialogue.

Mime is, in fact, one of the most versatile aids for emotionally entering the text, and can be done at any point in the discussion, sometimes requiring less than five minutes. Do give people a chance afterward, however, to jot down their reactions in their notebooks or journals, or to share verbally.

Do Role Play. While not as safe as mime, role play is easy for people to do and can be helpful as a way of bringing a story to life. You might try it with blind Bartimaeus (Mark 10:46-52 par.), the parable of the prodigal son (Luke 15:11-32), or the parable of the friend at midnight (Luke 11:5-8). With the latter, for instance, you might ask for two volunteers to act out the last part of the parable, with one knocking on the door and the other on the far side of the door (in another room) "sleeping" and resisting opening until he or she cannot stand it any longer. This can be absolutely delightful, and says volumes about the kind of energy which is required for intercessory prayer.

Role play can also be used to catch the mood of just one part of a story. In the middle of a discussion of the healing of the paralytic (Mark 2:1-12), for example, you might ask for four volunteers to be the paralytic's friends, and to show us how they would go about making a hole in the roof and lowering him down. The rest of us, in the meantime, can become those below, on whom the debris is raining, shaking our fists and shouting at them to stop. The whole interlude might take only three minutes, but it can bring the whole narrative suddenly to life in a way that mere talk could never do.

Role playing has this drawback, however: people can get so caught up in the role they have taken on that they find it difficult to come out of it afterward. For this reason it is essential that people be de-roled, so that their identification with their character is terminated. This can be done by having them talk about how they felt doing the role and what they learned from it. And avoid casting people in roles (such as that of the paralytic in the previous example) in which they could be inundated by an upsurge of unconscious contents. But careful de-roling will normally break any overidentification with the roles people play.

Role plays of the biblical story are not, it should be stressed, application exercises. They help people enter into the narrative but do not trace out its implications for us today. This is one of the most frequent confusions that I have observed over the years. Anything you do to enliven people's understanding of the text is a plus. But understanding the text is not enough. We must apply it to our own personal and social situation today. If you do a role play of the text, you will still need to provide some kind of application exercise.

Make up Skits. These are like role play but cast in contemporary terms. I have seen groups do hilarious retellings of the parable of the talents (Matt. 25:14-30 par.), or Jesus' resurrection appearance to the fishermen in John 21:1-14. For variety you might divide your group into four subgroups and have one do the text as a farce, one as a pantomime, one as a medieval mystery, one as serious drama, and compare the differences.

Work with Clay. This belongs by itself, both because of the technical problems (it's messy; people need to be in casual clothes; there must be a way to clean up without stopping up the plumbing), and because the experience is often of a different order from painting. Real clay is best; it hardens and can be taken home and kept in sight for further reflection. Play-Doh can be used in some settings (it's less messy, and also hardens). You could end the story of the healing of the paralytic (Mark 2:1-12) by having people do their own "inner paralytic" in clay. Encourage them to shut their eyes as they work, and let their hands make something, glancing at what they've done occasionally to see what is beginning to take shape. The hands have a wisdom the mind does not know. Then, after twenty minutes or so, the group reassembles and shares, together or in smaller groups, what they have discovered about themselves. Often a clay object will seem meaningless until its maker begins to speak; then suddenly it all comes together and the insight dawns.

Gestalt Characters. The basic idea is to enter imaginatively into the skin of another person or object and see yourself from that perspective. An example was given in chapter 3. By actually placing chairs opposite each other (or standing in two spots opposite each other, or even writing a dialogue), we can gain remarkable objectivity about how the other feels about us, and understand why. Then by shifting back and forth between the chair designated "me" and the chair designated "the other," we can move our own inner attitude toward genuine forgiveness and reconciliation. Having gained this objectivity and understanding, we can now go have an actual conversation with that person, if it seems appropriate, for now there is a real basis for actual reconciliation.

Repeat Holy Sentences (Mantras). As a way of deepening the meaning of a text, you might suggest that people walk around, ignoring one another, continually repeating to themselves or aloud a key line or phrase from the text. The phrase should be brief, preferably seven or eight syllables. We have used phrases from the Lord's Prayer (Luke 11:1-4; Matt. 6:7-13), or the words, "The Holy Spirit will teach you what to say" (Luke 12:12). On another occasion, after studying the story of the woman taken in adultery (John 8: 1-11), we walked around outside (it was night) repeating aloud, "Neither do I condemn you." After ten minutes we reconvened and walked around the room saying the same phrase to one another.

Move to Music. Select music that corresponds to the mood of the text, and ask people to move to it spontaneously, expressing the action (here you might give them bits of the scene to enact), the emotions present in the text, or their own emotional responses to it. This is *not* dancing. People can be awkward or inhibited and still express feelings which have been elicited by the text but have not yet found expression. This gives the right hemisphere of the brain a means for doing its own "exegesis," and involves much more of the total person. Often the left hemisphere is "humiliated" by such activity; that is just the medicine it needs.

Perform Physical Actions. Perhaps even more deliberate physical acts are called for, such as shouting the Lord's Prayer at the top of one's lungs, in order to experience, by exaggeration, what an energizing prayer it really is. In a retreat setting it can be valuable to ask each person to find a "place of power," and to build there an altar out of natural things. Perhaps they might attempt to include some symbol that speaks to them of wholeness, so that they can return to this spot after each session, bringing to it what has been uncovered in them as needing healing or challenge.

Paraphrase the Text. This can be especially effective with the overfamiliar passages. Ask people to rewrite, in their own words, the whole of the Lord's Prayer, *using no theological language,* and share what they have written in an atmosphere of meditation. Or have them paraphrase the commandment to love God with all our heart, soul, strength, and mind (Mark 12:28-31 par.), so as to say, again without theological crutches, what it is we mean, in plain language, by the word "God."

Subgroup Around a Key Question. In order to give everyone a chance to get in on an issue, you might divide the group into subgroups of from three to five persons and give them a question to struggle with together. With the story of the woman with the ointment, for example, you might ask subgroups to discuss the question, How do we contribute to systemic sexism today, especially in the church, and what do we intend to do about it? Or with the temptation narrative (Matt. 4:1-11), subgroups can share which of the three temptations is most characteristic of them as persons involved in helping others.

Form Dyads. Pair people off; have one ask the other a question over and over for two minutes. After each answer, the partner repeats the question. Or have the answerer say the same phrase over and over, completing it differently each time. After two or three minutes, reverse. Then have the pairs give each other feedback on what they heard. (See chapter 9, pages 140-41, questions on the healing of the woman with the hemorrhage, for an example.)

Write a Prayer. This can be a closing expression of what has come out of the study, or a request to God to deal with a specific need identified by the text. These prayers can be shared aloud or kept private, depending on their content. (See chapter 9, page 142, questions on the healing of blind Bartimaeus, for an example.)

Write a Parable, a Psalm, or a Poem. At the close of seminars on Jesus' parables of the Kingdom, you might invite people to write their own parables of the Kingdom and share them. After working with the Psalms, ask them to write their own psalms and share them in a setting of worship. In working with the Magnificat (Luke 1:46-55), ask people to spread out, shut their eyes, and move what it feels like to be mighty, proud, and rich; then what it feels like to be lowly, poor, and hungry. Then ask them to write their own Magnificat. It is astonishing how much sheer creativity is latent in a group of very average people—and no one is more astonished that it is there than those who discover it in the act of writing their psalms or parables. It may be helpful to lead people up to the act of writing by a meditative "journey" to a place of exquisite quietness and peace, so that they can release their creativity free from self-censure and self-consciousness.

Read Poetry. At Four Springs I was profoundly affected when Sheila Moon read her poems about Jesus, *Joseph's Son,*[4] standing in the center of a field at dusk. We had spread out at various distances around her with our backs to the center, looking out, so that we would be less inhibited about being seen as we moved. She read each poem once while we listened, motionless. Then she read it again as we moved to it. At the end of each poem we sat on the ground and jotted into our journals how we had felt, what we had perceived about Jesus and his journey. When the experience was over we shared whatever we wished. Since many of her poems deal with specific stories in the Gospels, a single poem might be paired with its text and used thus at the end of a session.

Develop Spontaneous Rituals. The group would need to develop this itself. After studying the Last Supper

(Mark 14:22-26 par.), for example, the group might want to design an agape meal together, or a eucharist, or a simple sharing of bread and wine. Once, after a session on the imprisonment of Paul and Silas in Philippi (Acts 16:11-40), the group learned the spiritual "Keep your eyes on the prize." Then members of the group spontaneously recalled those who are today suffering imprisonment and torture for their beliefs. After each remembrance, we sang together, as our prayer for their release and the doing of justice in their cause:

> Paul and Silas bound in jail
> Had no money for to go their bail
> Keep your eyes on the prize, hold on.
> Hold on, hold on!
> Keep your eyes on the prize, hold on.

If your group is not sufficiently aware of the proportions of such arrests, this could be a good time to introduce them to Amnesty International. Take time to have each of them read a different case history of torture and confinement, and then share it with the group between choruses.

Use Guided Meditations. At the close of a session, a leader might take the group back through the story, eyes closed, permitting time for people to feel into the story, perhaps as one of the characters. Or the group itself might meditatively lift up the words or phrases in the story that struck them most deeply, as for example in the story of the raising of Lazarus in John 11:1-54.

Paint Your Life-line. After studying the Synoptic passages on God's providence (Luke 13:1-5; Matt. 10:29-31/Luke 12:6-7; Matt. 6:25-34/Luke 12:22-31; Mark 10:29-30), people can draw on large newsprint the history of their experience of God's providence: all those points in their lives when they have experienced God's effective presence and power in blessing or tragedy. Then they share these in small groups. On another occasion, after working with Stephen's long revisionist history of God's dealings with Israel in Acts 6:8–8:3, people charted their own sacred history on large newsprint, as far back as they had to go, in order to trace their own spiritual roots. They were to list all the names and events, from "Adam and Eve" right up through their own birth and development, that have gone into making them who they are, spiritually. These are fascinating when shared.

Work with Two Sets of Texts. In attempting to apply Jesus' teaching to contemporary social issues, it may be helpful to juxtapose with the biblical text another, contemporary text. Our world is sometimes just too different to read directly off the text of the modern situation. If we can find the right match-up of biblical and current texts, however, we can establish a "dynamic analogy" (in James A. Sanders' phrase), which may throw light in *both* directions, helping us to see our own situation in a new way, and enabling us to glimpse dimensions of the text otherwise lost to view.

For example, with the parable of the laborers in the vineyard (Matt. 20:1-16) you might use Richard Sennett and Jonathan Cobb's *Hidden Injuries of Class* (New York: Vintage Books, 1973). Following an analysis of the parable and its exploration of God's grace and our feeling that we have to "earn" our way into life, you can give a brief (ten to twenty minute) summary of the way the Boston factory workers interviewed by Sennett and Cobb experience themselves as inadequate, unworthy, and inferior, and how the structure of the economic system operates invisibly to reinforce and perpetuate these feelings. You might conclude with the questions: How would you communicate the good news of God's unconditional love to these largely secular workers who nevertheless feel they must justify themselves somehow by works in order to "be somebody"? And what happens when we speak to them of God's acceptance without at the same time unmasking the way the system is structured to aggravate these feelings of unworthiness?

Other combinations of texts I have found potent are:

—The rich young man (Mark 10:17-31) and Ron Sider's *Rich Christians in an Age of Hunger* (New York: Paulist Press, and Downers Grove, Ill.: Intervarsity Press, 1977), using for example his sub-chapter, "Why Are Bananas Cheaper than Apples?" (pp. 163-65). In fact, one could do an entire series using just this book, since Sider has himself juxtaposed biblical and contemporary data throughout the book.

—The parable of the rich man and Lazarus (Luke 16:19-31) can be joined to materials on the inequities of the world economic system, using Sider, or a current videotape or slideshow. Jesus' teaching on nonviolence (Matt. 5:38-42) might be paired with Richard Attenborough's film *Gandhi*, for example; or the sayings on the way of the cross (Mark 8:34-35 par.) might be studied in conjunction with the Marlon Brando classic, *On the Waterfront*. The possibilities are endless.

—The feeding of the five thousand (Mark 6:30-44 par.) and Jesus' teaching on meals (Luke 14:7-24) can be paired with Jack Nelson's *Hunger for Justice* (Maryknoll, N.Y.: Orbis Books, 1980), a study of the systemic nature of the problem of world hunger from a biblical perspective.

These examples represent only a sample of the possibilities available. The texts themselves may suggest many more. I cannot stress enough, however, that the exercise must serve the intention of the text. It cannot be a gimmick for involving people, or an activity that has only a superficial relationship to the text. The medium must *be* the message. If the group has gone off in a direction you did not anticipate, and your exercise is no longer appropriate, you will have to scrap it and either think up another one fast, or else throw the problem to the group and see if they can help you come up with one.

For our interest is not in titillating the group with warm fuzzy experiences, or getting people to know one another better, but in finding that subtle intersection between the text and our own life where the sparks fly, the insights are born, the corner is turned—where, in short, we encounter the living God addressing us at the point of our and the world's need. To serve that end, and that end only, is the sole justification of these exercises.

Chapter 9

Sample Questions on Biblical Texts

Now we are at last ready to pull all the diverse pieces of this approach together, and to observe how each part functions in the whole. I need hardly add that the questions that I have provided in this chapter are by no means definitive. It has been extraordinarily hard for me even to finalize them for publication, since they change to some extent every time I use them. I have not even been able to conceive a full-fledged application exercise for all of them—though I have in every case asked questions of contemporary relevance. They are offered only as a help in learning what kinds of questions might profitably be asked. You may find it useful to read through them in order to get a sense of what they are struggling toward. If you are preparing to lead a group, *remember not to consult them until you have prepared your own preliminary set of questions.* Otherwise you may be seduced into following just my lead, rather than discovering your own questions—and some of these questions simply will not fit you. Once you have done your own work, *then* try them on for size, and feel free to use as many as make sense to you.

I have arranged the passages in topical blocks, since it is often best to begin with a fairly short series. Bible study need not be done on a single theme, however; you may want to select passages from the lectionary, or on the basis of their potential impact on the participants, or simply because you can handle certain texts more readily than others.

Remember to try to balance, better than I have done, concern for both the personal and the social.

Jesus on the Law

Eating with Sinners (Records ¶ 30; Parallels 53—Mark 2:13-17 par.)
1. Who were tax (or toll) collectors? Why were they

disreputable? Who would have been included in the term "sinners"?

2. Why did the religious authorities not eat with sinners? What does eating together imply? What is the psychological basis for the fear of defilement?
3. Why does Jesus associate with such people?
4. Why don't we?
5. One of the most radical aspects of Jesus' ministry was his association with the marginalized and outcast. Who are these people in our society today? Why are we afraid to associate with them? How might they "defile" us? How might we begin to relate to them?
6. Can you get in touch with the "sinner," the "tax collector," the "defiled" part of you? What keeps it from "coming to the table"?
7. Can you get in touch with the "Pharisee" in you? How does it feel about the defiled part of you? How does it treat it? What kinds of things does it say?
8. What in Jesus allowed him to associate with sinners? What does this say about his relation to his own inner darkness—his inner sinner and Pharisee?
9. Write a dialogue between your own inner sinner and your inner Pharisee. At some point have Jesus enter the conversation and invite your sinner-part to break bread with him. Record the dialogue. See if you can get your Pharisee to sit down at the table too.

On Fasting (*Records* ¶ 31; *Parallels* 54—Mark 2:18-22 par.)
1. What is the earliest recoverable form of this story? Compare Gospel of Thomas 104; Isa. 58:1-8.
2. Why do John's disciples and the Pharisees fast? What was to become later Christian practice?
3. What does Jesus imply by his answer? Is he forbidding fasting? What is the criterion for fasting? (Compare Matt. 6:16-18.)
4. What made the first person fast? Why did Jesus fast in the wilderness? What are the possible benefits of fasting? In removing fasting from the realm of custom and law, what is Jesus doing with it?

5. Is Jesus the bridegroom? Is this in its earliest form a metaphor or an allegory? In its earliest form is this a christological statement? What is the "wedding"?
6. What is the point of the little parables in 21-22? How does it tie in with 18-20? How do we continue to sew new patches on old garments or pour new wine into old wineskins?
7. Who among you has fasted? Share its meaning for you. How might we use fasting as an aid in our spiritual journeys or intercessions? (Suggest that some of them might try fasting in the coming week and possibly share the experience at the next meeting.)
8. Who are the people you know who have entered on public fasts today? Why have they done so? What is the connection between inner purification and social action? Is such fasting coercive?
9. Is there anything about which you care so deeply that you would consider fasting for it for a day? Three days? Seven? Twenty-one? Imagine that you are just completing a seven-day fast over that issue. Write an account of the spiritual (and physical) insights that have come to you in the process of your fast.

Plucking on the Sabbath (*Records* ¶ 32; *Parallels* 69—Mark 2:23-28 par.)
1. What is the charge brought to Jesus? What significance do you attach to the fact that it is the disciples, not Jesus, who are accused? Is the issue religious or economic?
2. What is his defense? Does it meet their objection? How does Matthew change it?
3. Explain the absence of vs. 27 of Mark in Matthew and Luke. What do you think is the original core of the narrative?
4. What is the basis for action on the Sabbath? Why did the first person keep the Sabbath? What was its purpose? Does Jesus make "man the measure of all things"? Does he make *himself?* Why doesn't Jesus take up the comparison with David and conclude, "So the Son of *David* is lord even of the Sabbath"? Does Jesus appeal to

his own authority, or to a principle inherent in the situation? In the material that Matthew adds, is appeal made to Jesus' authority or to a principle inherent in the situation?

5. Is this license? What attitude does Jesus take toward the Sabbath here?

6. Look at the variant for Luke 6:5 from Codex Bezae. What is the principle of discrimination? How can we become the kind of persons who know what we are doing?

7. Who or what then is the "son of man" here? Is it Jesus? How would our decisions be affected if we were related to this "son of man"? The "son of man" might bring what to our decisions?

8. What do you learn about Jesus here?

9. Do a walking mantra or holy sentence. Walk around outside or inside for ten minutes, repeating over and over, "The Son of Man is lord even of _____." Examples: my sexuality, my children, my job, etc. You may want to retranslate the phrase in a less sexist way: "The Human Being is sovereign even over _____.") When you return, spend a few minutes journaling about what it would mean for the Human Being to really be the ultimate value in every aspect of your life.

The Man with the Withered Hand (*Records* ¶ 33; *Parallels* 70—Mark 3:1-6 par.)

1. How is Mark's account different from Luke's? From Matthew's? Why do you think Mark doesn't have Matthew 12:11-12? Why do Matthew and Luke not have the reference to Jesus' anger? What two forms of stories come together here?

2. Apparently a fuller event has been so condensed that the healing has almost become a foil for the teaching here. Allowing for that, try to place yourself in the story as Mark describes it. Where are you? What day is it? How do you and the others regard people like this man with a withered hand? How does Jesus heal him?

3. What is the meaning of Jesus' question, "Is it lawful?" Does he reject the law? Does he break it here?

4. What is the reaction of the Pharisees? Who are the "Herodians"? Why are the Pharisees willing to link up with the Herodians to kill him after this? Why would the Herodians want him killed? What has been evoked by Jesus that these forces want to kill?
5. What is it about Jesus' sense of justice that the authorities don't understand? At what point does the duty to comply with laws cease to be binding, in view of the need to help others or to oppose injustice? How is this liberating power manifesting itself in us today as we relate to the power structures of society?
6. Now, close your eyes, and envision that you are:

(a) Jesus coming into the synagogue on the Sabbath. You walk in and see a man sitting there with a deformed hand. You know your enemies are all around you waiting for a chance to find fault with you. The man on the bench hasn't asked you for anything. Nonetheless, you call him over, ask him to stretch out his withered hand, and he is healed. Your enemies leave to plot against you.

(b) One of the Pharisees. You too enter the synagogue right behind this pretentious preacher from Galilee. You too see the cripple on the bench. You know Jesus can heal him, but if he does he will have broken the sabbath law against work. Jesus reminds you that the importance of life supersedes the law, and calls the man to him. The man exposes his crippled hand, and it is cured in front of your eyes. You leave to plot against Jesus.

(c) The crippled man sitting on the bench in the synagogue waiting for the service to begin. Your withered, useless hand is resting in your lap. Because of it you can't do heavy work. Life is difficult. Suddenly a commotion occurs at the door, and a stranger comes in followed by a group of Pharisees. They start talking about healing on the sabbath. Suddenly the stranger turns to you and calls you over to where the group is standing. You go. "Stretch out your hand," he says, "show us your crippled part." And suddenly your hand is no longer crippled.

7. How did you feel as Jesus?—as the Pharisee?—as the cripple? Which did you identify with the most? Why?

8. Why does Jesus make the man display his withered hand? Why must we display our "withered parts" in order to be healed?

9. Distribute a piece of clay to each participant. Have each make the "withered part" within (15-20 minutes). Share in whole group or smaller subgroups.

On Loving One's Enemies (*Records* ¶ 37 H, L-R; *Parallels* 27—Matt. 5:43-48 / Luke 6:27-28, 32-36)

After both Matthew and Luke have been read:

1. Where was it said, "You shall love your neighbor and hate your enemy"? Read Lev. 19:17-18; 33-34; Exod. 23:4-5 (compare Deut. 22:4). Is Jesus promulgating a new law? What is he doing with the tradition? How has this sentence been used to foster anti-Semitism?

2. What makes people our enemies? Are there aspects of yourself that you treat like an enemy?

3. What happens when we love our enemy? Does the enemy cease to be our enemy? Why, according to Jesus, are we to love our enemy?

4. What is God like, according to Jesus? Is this the way most people view God or reality? What kind of world would we have if God did *not* cause the sun to rise on the evil and on the good?

5. What is the new thing that Jesus is saying about God here, that goes beyond the way we normally regard God? Why does Jesus make the nature of God the basis for how we should treat our enemies?

6. Compare Matt. 5:48 with Luke 6:36. Which do you think best sums up the point of the whole paragraph? What has been the effect of "Be ye therefore perfect" on you? How else could Matthew's "perfect" be translated? One possible translation is "all-inclusive." What is the difference between being "perfect" and being "all-inclusive"? What does "all-inclusive" imply about the nature of God?

7. When we try to be perfect, what do we do with our imperfections? How does perfectionism affect our capacity to love our enemies, inside and out?
8. What quality or characteristic is most difficult for you to accept in yourself? Who is the enemy within? (Suggest that each person write down answers and share.) What would it mean for us to be "all-inclusive" toward ourselves? Toward others? What effect would taking this seriously have on the issue of disarmament? On our relationship with Communist countries?

On Judging (Records ¶ 38F, I: Parallels 36—Matt. 7:1-5/Luke 6:37-38, 41-42)
1. List rapidly on a piece of paper all the things you don't like about someone. Set it aside.
2. What is Jesus saying here about judging? Is he saying that we shouldn't judge? What is he warning against? (Compare Matthew and Luke.)
3. What is the relationship between the log and the splinter? Why must we begin by dealing with the log?
4. Take out the list you made of things you don't like about someone, and put your *own* name beside the other's name, and ask how many of the things you've listed are also true of you. Share. What are we doing when we see aspects of ourselves in others?
5. Why do we project onto others? Is projection "bad"? What is its value?
6. What in this context does Jesus mean by "hypocrite"? What does this statement say we can do with others after we have worked on ourselves?
7. Relating all this to the previous passage, why do we need our enemies? What can our enemy do for us that nobody else can do? What can the Soviets teach us about ourselves?

On Anger (Records ¶ 37A; Parallels 22—Matt. 5:21-24)
1. What was the old law? What is the new thing that Jesus is saying in contrast to the old?

2. What have been the consequences through Christian history of this injunction not to be angry? What have been the consequences for you personally?
3. How would it change the way you perceived this text if we used the NEB translation, "Anyone who *nurses* anger ... must be brought to judgment"? (The present participle suggests continuous action in the present.)
4. If we took that translation as our guide, then, Jesus might be suggesting that we deal with anger how?
5. Compare Eph. 4:26-27 RSV and NEB. What does it say about how we are to deal with anger? What does it say about being angry or nursing anger? Why does letting the sun go down on our anger give opportunity to the devil?
6. Back to Matthew. When you are offering your gift, who has the grievance? What does that suggest about the initiative for reconciliation?
7. What is the content of "altar" for you? What is different because of going to the altar? How is the process of reconciliation going to be different because the altar is a part of it? Why is it before the altar that this need for reconciliation comes to awareness?
8. Exercise (see chapter 3, pages 58-59) and feedback.

Parables of God's Reign

The Parable of the Sower (*Records* ¶ 47 A-F; *Parallels* 90—Mark 4:1-9 par.)
1. Look first at the refrains in Mark 4:9, 23, 24; Matt. 13:18, 43. What does this warning lead you to expect about Jesus' teaching about the Kingdom (even if some of these have been added)? What were the current Jewish expectations about the Kingdom? With what colors would you describe it? What gestures?
2. Identify with the sower.[1] What then would the parable say to you? (Ask people to be specific and make "I" statements.)
3. Identify with the soil. Where is this beaten-down path in you? What is it that keeps us from hearing the new word that we need to hear?

(You might have people scatter around the room and physically act out being each of these soils in turn. Then share in pairs in what ways we felt our lives were like each of these soils.)

4. Can you locate the rocky soil in yourself?
5. What are your thorns?
6. In almost all of Jesus' parables there is something incongruous, something that doesn't fit, or is surprising, or beyond possibility. Here it is the return, which was normally five-fold. What is he saying about this soil? Do you know this soil in yourself? Are you in touch with the reality of this fruitfulness?
7. At which point does this parable find you out—as sower, or as one of the soils? Where does it resonate most in you? What does it say to you?
8. What does this parable suggest about the nature of God's Reign?[2] How does it contrast with current expectations of its coming? What does it imply about the nature of God?

The Interpretation of the Parable of the Sower (Records ¶ 47 L-P: Parallels 93—Mark 4:13-20 par.)
1. Compare this interpretation with the parable. How do they differ? In the parable, people are represented by what? In the interpretation the seed is what in Mark vs. 14? What is the seed in Mark vs. 15? 16? 18? 20? At the end of vs. 15 the people are what? How do you account for these discrepancies?
2. What is the point of the interpretation? At what points does it allegorize the parable?[3]

The Reason of Speaking in Parables (Records ¶ 47 G-J; Parallels 91—Mark 4:10-12 par.)
1. What are the differences between Mark and Matthew/Luke?
2. What, according to Mark, keeps the people from hearing? What, according to Matthew?
3. Does Jesus tell parables in order to prevent hearing, or does their hardness of heart prevent their hearing? Does he wish to be understood, or not understood? Why then

does he use parables? (See John Dominic Crossan, *In Parables* [New York: Harper & Row, 1973]).
4. What is indicated about developments in the church by the expression "those outside"?

The Parable of the Seed Growing Secretly (Records ¶ 48 D: Parallels 95—Mark 4:26-29)
1. (Compare Gospel of Thomas 21. Mark 4:29 may be a free-floating saying from Joel 3:13 added to give the parable an eschatological thrust.)
2. What is this parable getting at? Where is the seed sown? What does that feel like in you? What is Jesus saying about God's Reign here?
3. How would this contrast with Jewish expectations? With our talk of "building the Kingdom"?

The Parable of the Mustard Seed (Records ¶ 48 E; Parallels 97—Mark 4:30-32)
1. What are the differences among the three Gospels? Compare Gospel of Thomas 20. Which is Thomas closer to?
2. Look at Ezek. 17:22-24; Dan. 4:10-12, 20-22. In those the cedar of Lebanon represents what? Why did Jesus use mustard instead of the cedar of Lebanon?
3. In the parable, which do you think was original, "shrub" or "tree"? Where does "tree" come from?
4. What is a mustard plant like? How does this parable contrast to the Jewish expectations of the Kingdom?
5. What is God's Reign like, then, in your own words?
6. What are the social implications of this view of God's Reign?

The Parable of the Leaven (Records ¶ 48 F; Parallels 98—Matt. 13:33 par.)
1. Compare Gospel of Thomas 96. (Note this rule: The kingdom of heaven is not like *leaven*, or like a *woman*, but rather it is like the following *picture*.)
2. How is bread leavened? How much is three measures?

Why "hid"? Why does Jesus choose this image to speak of God's Reign? Why does he use as his model a woman?
3. How does this contrast with Jewish expectations?
4. What does this mean socially? Personally? What would it mean for your growth if you really knew this leaven was working in you?
5. In what societies, among what groups, do you see this leaven rising today?

The Lost Coin (Records ¶ 105 C; Parallels 172—Luke 15:8-9 only)
1. What is symbolized by the lost coin? The dark house? The lamp? What seems to you to be the meaning of the parable?
2. Write on a piece of paper: What have I lost? (Or, What is the lost coin in me?) (Perhaps share.)
3. What would it mean for me to light a lamp and sweep the house and seek diligently until I find it?

The Parables of the Hidden Treasure and of the Pearl (Records ¶ 48 N-O; Parallels 101—Matt. 13:44-46)
1. Why is the treasure hidden in the field? How does the man discover it? Is the owner of the treasure still alive? Why doesn't the man just take it? What would happen if he suddenly started spending it? What would he have to sell?
2. "In his joy"—can you get into his feeling? Is "selling all" a sacrifice? Why is God's Reign like this? What does it mean to sell all? What would it mean for you to sell all?
3. The Pearl: What do pearls symbolize? Where do they come from? What for you is the Pearl for which you could sell all? Why is God's Reign like this story?
4. List on paper the things you would most hate to give up. Then ask out of what "sheer joy" you could gladly relinquish which things on your list. Which could you not? Then ask what "selling all" means in reference to your list. Break into small groups and share.

Summary of Parables
1. Where are the seeds? The leaven? The coin? The treasure? The pearl? What is the significance of the fact

that in all these parables God's Reign is compared to something hidden, lost, buried? How does this "feminine" imagery contrast with the way the Kingdom was usually symbolized? With what colors would you describe the Reign of which Jesus is speaking? What gestures? What does this suggest about the nature of God's Reign and how it comes? How do we get related to it then?

2. What do these parables reveal about Jesus? About the nature of God? About God's Reign? What are the political implications of Jesus' view of God's Reign?

Exercises:
1. Write a parable. Share. (Prepare people through a guided meditation so that they don't just try to illustrate some theological ideas.)
2. Gestalt the parable of the treasure or the lost coin—be each part of the parable in turn (field, treasure, farmer, the realtor, the "all" he sold; or the woman, lost coin, lamp, broom, house).

The Parable of the Two Sons (Records ¶ 129 A-B; Parallels 203—Matt. 21:28-32)
1. What relationship with the father did the son have who said yes and then didn't go?
2. What relationship to the father did the son have who said no and went?
3. What two options are not included here? Why are they not included?
4. In a patriarchal society, how would Jesus' hearers have reacted to hearing that the son said no to his father? Did you ever say no to yours? Why might it be important to say no to God? What kind of relationship with God would be required?
5. To whom was this parable apparently addressed? What groups or classes are symbolized by the two sons (a) in Jesus' day, (b) in ours? Who are those today who have said no and yet "do the will of the father"?
6. How does it make you feel that the "tax collectors and harlots" are the first to enter the kingdom? Given a choice between the chief priests and elders, on the one hand, and

the tax collectors and harlots on the other, with which group do you naturally identify?

7. Why does God want our capacity to say no as a precondition for our obedience? What happens when we bring only the yes and deny that the no exists in us altogether? Why does Jesus not make the "yes, yes" response the model for discipleship, as the church has? What does bringing all our ambivalence to God do for choice?

8. Exercise: Pair off by size, face each other, lock fingers and hands with arms extended, and lean into each other, the one repeating "No I won't!", the other responding "Yes you will!" After a few moments, reverse roles.

9. How did you feel saying no? To whom were you really saying it? Why does God want our noes?

10. Can you share out of your own life experience ways you said no to God that enabled a greater yes?

The Parable of the Ten Maidens (Records ¶ 136 E; Parallels 227—Matt. 25:1-13)

1. This parable occurs within the whole block of material dealing with the unexpected arrival of the Judgment (Matthew 24-25). Further, the parable includes a tag ending (vs. 13), which easily locates it in this context. The church from its earliest days has usually interpreted this parable as an allegory. How would you set up the allegorical equations?

    wedding =
    bridegroom =
    bride (offstage) =
    the bridegroom's delay =
    wise maidens =
    foolish maidens =
    oil for lamps =
    the shut door =
    sleeping =

2. How then does the tag ending of vs. 13 (also found in Matt. 24:36, 42, 44, 50 in various forms) sum up the meaning allegorically?

3. Yet if vs. 13 is taken as a summary of the parable, how do we account for the fact that all ten maidens fall asleep? In what sense (if any) is one group more "watchful" than the other? Why is the bride not even mentioned?

4. If vs. 13 is set aside as an inappropriate tag ending, imported to this place by Matthew, it is possible to see this story as a genuine parable. The details reflect actual wedding customs. The groom and his male retinue would fetch the bride in the evening after the bride price had been agreed on. But distance, or haggling over the bride price, could delay their return to the wedding feast. The task of the maidens was to provide light for the banquet. And once everyone was at the feast, the door was apparently shut in order to keep evil spirits out. (Weddings still attract the largest number of superstitious practices of any rite in our society as well.)

   When the bridegroom finally comes, why do the wise maidens refuse to share their oil?

   When the foolish maidens return with their oil, why are they refused entrance?

5. What is the parable saying about God's Reign? What is it like? What is the symbolism of midnight? Oil? The wedding?

6. What does it mean for us today, "The door is shut"? Where do we see it shutting? For whom is it shut?

7. How do we behave like these foolish maidens, both personally and socially? Why does the bridegroom say, "I do not know you"?

8. What would be required of us to be like the wise maidens today? If all the maidens sleep, what does it mean to be ready to celebrate the coming of God's Reign? What kind of God is pictured here?

9. Paint the closed door. Write a meditation on your picture.

The Parable of the Talents (Records ¶ H-Q; Parallels 228—Matt. 25:14-30/Luke 19:12-27)

1. Compare the accounts. Which strikes you as more authentic, three servants or ten? The larger amount of

money or the smaller? Equal shares or unequal? The master as a merchant or a king? Matthew's ending, or Luke's? What seems to be the original core of the parable?

2. You might do playlets or skits, placing the story in a contemporary setting.
3. What is "it" in Matthew vs. 14?
4. The master is joyful over the two servants who do what? He is upset over the one who does what? Why does the master reward the ones who risked everything? What does God want from us?
5. What was the view of the master the first two servants had that enabled them to risk? What was the third servant's view of the master? How does the master respond to the third servant's view? Does he agree with it? (Note the question mark, Matthew vs. 26 par.)
6. Imagine God conceived much as the third servant regarded his master. How might this God be disappointed in you? Now imagine God conceived much as the first and second servants regarded their master. How might this affect your behavior and self-attitude? How might this God be disappointed in you? What might it mean to "enter into the joy" of such a master? With which view of God do you really function most of the time?
7. What is symbolized by the money? (Note: A "talent" here refers to a coin, not to our abilities.) What is it that God wants from us?
8. What happens to God when we fail to augment God's "money"? The mystic Jacob Boehme once said, "God is the Nothing that wants to become Something." Elsewhere he speaks of the "famished will of God," which only we can feed by our response. In the light of these statements and the text, what would you say is the "wrath of God"?
9. What have you buried? Do a guided meditation in which people imagine themselves digging in a field, searching for and finding this lost part of themselves, and embracing it back into themselves.
10. Paint or write a dialogue with the "God in your guts," the negative God of the third servant, the Shadow God who is

out to get you. Discuss with partners what hold this image of God continues to have over you.

(Note: It is my view that the "talents" in this parable do not symbolize what we today call "talents," that is, our most developed capacities, but rather the whole self, including— perhaps especially including—those undeveloped and inferior functions and aspects which we have neglected or rejected. In the history of interpretation the "talents" have been increasingly narrowed, from a symbol of the whole self or untapped energies in the self, to the special gifts of the Holy Spirit, to our best natural "gifts," and finally to those abilities which have potential earning power in the economic sphere. Whether you agree or not, however, do try to move the discussions beyond platitudes about "developing our God-given talents." Everyone already believes in doing that, and leaving the issue there merely trivializes the parable.)

Jesus' Way of Healing

The Lawyer's Question and the Parable of the Compassionate Samaritan (Records ¶ 83; Parallels 143-144—Luke 10:25-37; compare Matt. 22:34-40/Mark 12:28-31).

1. Compare the lawyer's question in Matthew, Mark, and Luke. How do you account for the differences?
2. What is the lawyer asking Jesus? How do we ask the same question?
3. Who answers the question? Which do you think is more original—that Jesus answered or the lawyer?
4. Where is the answer from? Take out a piece of paper and write, *What* is it that we are to love with all our heart, soul, mind, and strength—using *no theological terms*. That is to say, what, in everyday language, do you mean by "God"? (Five minutes. Share without commenting on.)
5. What does it mean to "love your neighbor as yourself"? Throughout Christian history, how has that generally been heard? Why love your neighbor *as* yourself? What happens when we don't love ourselves?
6. What prompts the lawyer to ask, "And who is my neighbor?"

7. Now turn to the parable. Which direction is the journeyer going? The priest? Why might the priest be traveling? Why does he pass by? What would be the consequences for the priest if the man died on his hands? Read Lev. 21:1-3. What new light might it shed on the priest's dilemma if we know that he will be disbarred from the priesthood for life if the man dies in his hands?

8. Who were Levites? Samaritans?

9. Imagine yourself as each character in turn. Be the priest (describe the scene). As you approach, you feel . . . And as you pass by you feel . . . Next be the Levite . . . the wounded person . . . the Samaritan. (Or mime each character in turn. See pages 112-13 for instructions.)

10. Why is it the Samaritan who has compassion? Compassion literally means what? What is the source of compassion in us?

11. What happens when we call the Samaritan "good"? Does he stop because he's good, or do we call him good because he stops? We have generally assumed that compassion is taught how? How can compassion be learned?

12. The lawyer asked, "Who is my neighbor?" How does Jesus rephrase it at the end? Why? What is it that the lawyer cannot bring himself to say? What is Jesus trying to lead the lawyer to do about his racial prejudices?

13. Who are the "wounded" in our society today? Who are the "robbers"? Without getting sidetracked on the question of whether we should stop on the highway for disabled cars or hitchhikers, what would we bring to actual wounded people or groups of people if we were in touch with the wounded aspect in us?

14. Who is the "wounded person" in you? (Or, in Fritz Kunkel's terms, "When were you first killed?")

15. Paint your wounded inner part. (See chapter 8, pages 109-10 for fuller instructions.) Share (in whole group or in smaller groups).

The Woman with the Ointment (Records ¶ 42; Parallels 83—Luke 7:36-50)

1. Who is this woman? What can we know about her? What about her hair? The alabaster flask of ointment? Her touching Jesus? Her coming into this banquet of men and doing this?
2. Why do you think she comes to Jesus? She is expressing what attitude toward Jesus?
3. What is Jesus' response?
4. How does Simon respond to this intrusion? How does he feel about this woman? What most offends him? What is the source of his fear of defilement? Where does it come from in us?
5. What does the Pharisee think about Jesus? Why has he invited him?
6. How does Jesus want Simon to hear this little parable? In order to hear it, Simon would have to do what? What might become of him if he began to treat women the way Jesus does?
7. Does forgiveness result from love or create it?
8. What might become of this woman? (See Luke 8:1-3.)
9. On the basis of just this story, what would you say is the content of the word "faith," using no theological language?
10. Where do we see signs of systemic sexism in this story? How are we still practicing it today, especially in the church?
11. How do you feel about this woman? Who is she in you? What role does she have in coming to faith?
12. Write a dialogue between yourself and the woman. (See chapter 8, pages 110-12 for fuller instructions.)

The Healing of the Woman with a Spirit of Weakness (Records ¶ 98; Parallels ¶ 163—Luke 13:10-17)
1. Divide the group. Have half of them walk around bent over for five minutes, the other half erect and talking to the bent ones. Then reverse. Share how it felt.
2. What would it be like to have this for *eighteen years?* How was her problem diagnosed by her contemporaries? By Jesus?
3. How is she healed? In healing her, what social conventions does Jesus break?

4. Why does Jesus say, "You *are freed*" instead of "be freed," if she is "bound by Satan"? What does this story imply about Jesus' attitude toward healing?
5. Why does she praise God, not Jesus? How does healing take place, and what is our role in it?
6. To whom does the ruler of the synagogue protest (literally, "he was going around saying")? Why?
7. Why does Jesus say "hypocrites" when only the ruler of the synagogue has spoken?
8. Does Jesus' argument (or the early church's) really speak to the objection? Why does the Law make exception for animals but not for people? (Cf. Deut. 5:14.) What will become of the Sabbath if human needs are individualized like this?
9. Jesus calls her "Daughter of Abraham," a phrase found nowhere else in the Bible or anywhere else, so far as I can determine. What is he saying and doing by this?
10. In what ways do contemporary women feel bent over? Men?
11. Under what burden have you been bent for all these years? What is the "spirit of weakness" in you? Write on it for a few minutes.
12. What is the strength hidden in your weakness?
13. How can faith heal your "spirit of weakness"? What would it take for this part of us to become a "Daughter of Abraham"? Break into small groups and share.

The Healing of the Paralytic (Records ¶ 29; Parallels 52—Mark 2:1-12 par.)
1. Have four people volunteer to role play the four friends (for details on role playing, see pages 113-14).
2. For what purpose did the friends bring this man to Jesus? What evidence is there as to the attitude of the man himself?
3. What do they do when they can't reach Jesus? What did Jesus "see" that he identifies as "faith"? What evidence is there as to the attitude of the paralytic himself? What does it take to produce this kind of faith?

4. Why does Jesus speak of forgiveness? Do you think this is what the paralytic expected to hear? What connection might there be between sin and the man's paralysis?
5. Does Jesus forgive him? Who forgives? How do the scribes hear him? Are they correct? What is the penalty for blasphemy?
6. What is meant by "which is easier"? Which *is* easier?
7. Who or what is the "Son of man" here? Compare Matt. 9:8.
8. The paralytic could have simply walked out. What is added by "take up your bed"?
9. Taking the story within, who is the paralytic in you? What aspect of yourself needs the healing offered in this story? Who is the scribe in you? Why doesn't it want the paralytic healed—both in you and in the story? What is the relationship between the "scribe" and the "paralytic"? What would be involved in reconciling the two?
10. Who are these four "helpers"? What resources are available to bring us to the healing power?
11. Do your "paralytic" in clay. (See chapter 8, pages 114-15 for fuller instructions.)

The Woman with the Hemorrhage (Records ¶ 52 O-J; Parallels 107—Mark 5:24-34 par.)
(This passage can be introduced by a role play; parts will have to be rehearsed slightly so that key characters are familiar enough with their roles.)
1. In Mark, when is she healed? When is she healed in Luke? Matthew? If she was healed immediately upon touching Jesus, why does Matthew make it the consequence of Jesus' word to her? Why does Mark have vs. 34*b*? (Compare NEB.) As the tradition develops, what is happening to the relative roles of the woman and Jesus?
2. What is the woman suffering? What were the social consequences of bleeding? How do you think she felt about her body?
3. Why does she sneak up behind him in the crowd? What gives her the courage to touch him, if all other physicians have failed?

4. How would you account for her healing? List the possible explanations. (See Appendix 1.)
5. Why is the woman afraid (vs. 33)? What has she done to Jesus by touching him? Why does Jesus make her own up to what she's done? What does this add to her healing? Why must it be *public?*
6. What is "faith" as depicted in this story? Define it on the basis of what is in this story alone.
7. What is the role of Jesus in her healing, if it is *her* faith that healed her?
8. Divide into pairs. For two minutes one of you say to the other, "If I touch his garment, I shall be _____,"

   giving a different statement of your need for healing each time. After one gives as many answers as possible within the two minutes, reverse roles. (The leader should announce when the two minutes are up. Afterward give them some time to reflect with each other on what they heard themselves saying.)

Blind Bartimaeus (Records ¶ 21; *Parallels* 193—Mark 10:46-52 par.)
This passage can be effectively introduced by role play, with half the group at one end of a large room, half at the other. Have them all shut their eyes (stress not peeking) and be blind Bartimaeus. (Or use blindfolds.) Say: Cross the room blindly, go to your little hovel, lie down and sleep. Now the cock announces morning. You rise, put your mantle around you, and eat a crust of bread with water and, if you're lucky, salt. You leave your house, finding your way to the gate of Jericho (the other end of the room). You take your seat and spread your mantle to catch the coins thrown your way. A stander-by [the leader] asks, "Hey, Bart, what are you doing up so early?" (All the "Barts" answer.) The dialogue continues, with the stander-by ridiculing Bartimaeus for thinking Jesus would give him the time of day or could heal blindness. Then the stander-by says, "Hey, here comes a crowd. I bet it's your Jesus." The "Barts" begin to shout, and the leader tries to shush them up. Then, "Wait, Bart, he's calling you." They will get up and head for your voice. "Over here, Bart."

When they have all come, say, "Jesus wants to know what you want." They answer. Leader: "He says, Go your way, your faith has saved you." (This works better if you can get a second person to play the role of Jesus.)

1. Why do the disciples try to silence Bartimaeus' outcry? (How would the authorities hear "Son of David"?)
2. How does Jesus respond?
3. How do you account for the sudden change in the ones who silenced him? What is their relationship to Jesus?
4. Why does Jesus ask Bartimaeus what he wants? How do we sometimes cling to our problems? What does it take to be ready to be healed?
5. Jesus said to Bartimaeus, "Your faith has made you well." What evidence is there of Bartimaeus' faith? What would he probably have meant by "Son of David" in his Jewish context? Does he have faith because of, or in spite of, this affirmation? What is the nature of faith here?
6. What does Jesus tell Bartimaeus to do? What does he do? The early church called themselves simply "Followers of the Way." What might be the consequences of his choosing to follow Jesus now to Jerusalem?
7. On a sheet of paper, write out what it is that you want God to do for you. (This is made easier by the concluding exercise of the woman with the hemorrhage. These two passages are very effective when done together in the same session.) In the silence, ask: Do I really want it? Am I willing to pay the price?
8. Write out a prayer, telling God what you want, with all the brass and gusto of Bartimaeus. Trust God for it. Thank God in advance.

(This can serve as the climax of the series on healing, perhaps even leading into a healing liturgy, with the laying on of hands.)

The Principalities and Powers
Colossians 1:15-20

1. The context speaks of God's action in delivering us from "the dominion of darkness" and transferring us to the realm of God's beloved Son (1:13-14). Then follows

1:15-20, where the Powers that comprise this "dominion of darkness" are described as created by God in, through, and for Christ. How can they be both good creations and a dominion of darkness?

2. Play with the imagery of "in, through, and for." What does it mean that everything, the Powers included, is created *in* Christ? What images come to your imagination? *Through* Christ—again, what images? *For* Christ—what images? (Some of them may be feminine images; note the origin of much of the conception here in Sophia or Divine Wisdom, Prov. 8 and Wis. Sol. 7.)

3. These Powers are "in heaven and on earth, visible and invisible." Give examples of each. (You may find helpful my discussion in Part 3 of the book *Naming the Powers*.)

4. What are "thrones" (as opposed to the ruler who sits on them)? "Dominions" (or "territories")? "Principalities" (*archai*—"incumbents")? "Authorities" or "powers" (*exousiai*—legitimations and sanctions)?

5. What does it mean for faith that these Powers that comprise the dominion of darkness are, in their essence, good? That they all "hold together" in Christ? What is this saying about God's will for institutions, systems, and social structures? How do such systems become demonic? Can they be redeemed?

6. In the struggle against the "dominion of darkness," what is the difference between a view that regards the Powers as totally evil, and this one in Colossians, where they are created good but are fallen?

Ephesians 6:12
1. Why does the author say that we are *not* contending against human beings? Who or what then are we fighting against?
2. How does this insight help us love our human enemies?
3. Give examples of the diseased or demonic spirituality of some institution with which you are familiar.

Ephesians 2:1-3
1. Why does the author speak of believers as previously *dead?* What killed them?

    2. What is "the power of the air"? What are the things that are "in the air" that kill people spiritually today?

    3. Write a *reverse* Lord's Prayer, as an imprecation against the "god of this world" (2 Cor. 4:4) and its "dominion of darkness." (For example: "Tyrant, who reigns on earth, desecrated be your name. May your rule be broken and your will thwarted on earth by the power of heaven. Do not give us this day the blandishments by which you seduce us into complicity," etc.)

Colossians 2:13-15

    1. What has God had to do in order to make us, who were "dead," alive again? What happens when our understanding of salvation stops at forgiveness (vs. 13) and doesn't go on to the unmasking of the Powers? What is the difference between a personal doctrine of the atonement, and a social doctrine of the atonement (Christus Victor)?

    2. What has God done to the Powers through the cross? Are they rendered powerless? There are translation problems here; the best translation is probably the RSV, with "exposed" substituted for "disarmed." Note that Paul says that it is precisely the cross that accomplishes this exposure, not the resurrection (though it is not less essential for the victory, v. 13). What actually happened to the Powers as a result of Jesus' crucifixion? What in human history will never be the same again?

    3. Why is this victory described as a *present* fact, not a future event? What is the difference between believing that we must somehow overthrow a system like apartheid in South Africa, and believing that it has *already* been overthrown and is being led in Christ's triumphal procession?

Colossians 2:20

    1. What does it mean to "die out from under" the elemental Powers of the universe?

    2. Can you share how you have actually died to such Powers in the past?

3. Why, having experienced salvation, transformation, redemption, are we still in the grip of such Powers?

Ephesians 3:10
1. What, according to this passage, is the task of the Church with reference to the Powers?
2. Is it our task to overthrow them?
3. What is the power of truth in restoring the Powers to their created roles under God?

Exercises:
1. What Power most holds you in its thrall, keeping you from acting faithfully in the world?
2. Make that Power in clay. Or, go outside and find something which represents for you that Power.
3. In groups of three, share:
   a. Why do I give this Power so much power over my life?
   b. What would it take for me to die out from under this power?
4. Make a large placard naming the Power with which you are contending for freedom. Create a processional behind a cross, in which each person displays the name of the Power from which s/he is allowing God to free her/him, singing an appropriate hymn.
Close with prayer as all hold the placards high as a supplication to God for deliverance.

The Angels of the Churches (Revelation 1-3)
1. Someone read Rev. 1:9-20. What is the relationship between the seven churches and this figure in their midst? How can we assert that the Human Being is made manifest by churches as imperfect as these? What then is the task of the church?
2. Read Rev. 2:1-7. Outline the structure of the letter.
3. Read Rev. 2:8-11. Do you read the "your" in these letters as singular or plural? They are singular, with a few exceptions (2:10, 23-24). What then is the angel of a church? Why is John instructed to address these letters to the angel rather than the congregation, as did Paul?

4. Look at 2:10. Why does the plural "you" suddenly shift back to the singular in the last phrase ("I will give you [sing.] the crown of life")? How would it affect the way you underwent imprisonment if you knew that the whole congregation's "crown" was riding on your faithfulness? How would it affect your relationship to those in prison if you knew that your share in the crown depended on their faithfulness?

5. Individuals and the congregation as a whole are addressed in the body of the letters. Why then is the angel held accountable?

6. How would you describe the angel of a church in contemporary terms? What is it about the angel of a church that is more than the sum total of all its parts?

7. How does the angel of a church maintain its gestalt or personality over a period of time, even when there is a rapid turnover of members and even clergy? Describe the angel of a church you have known (not your current church).

8. What happens when we try to change a church without consulting its angel? How would we go about discerning its angel?

9. What is the role of the Human Being (or Son of Man) in changing the angel of a church? Of John?

10. If the angel is the interiority or "within" of a church, its spirituality or essence or corporate personality, then the outer manifestations of a church ought to reveal its inner reality. What are some of the visible attributes of the angel of a church, and what might they tell us about its angel? (List on newsprint.)

11. Take pencil and paper. Analyze the angel of your church, using this list (# 10) as a guide. Don't simply note the answer (e.g. racial make-up: Caucasian), but note *what this fact reveals about the angel of your church.* When you are finished, take some colors and do a picture of the angel of your church. Try to let the colors choose you. The pictures can be abstract, stick figures, or just pure colors. No one cares what they look like.

12. Share your pictures all together. Try to discern emerging common features.
13. Take pen and paper and go find a place in a room with enough space in front of you to fall down on your face. (Read Rev. 1:9-11a, stopping after "seven churches," and 12-17.) After vs. 17a, when all have fallen on their faces, say, "Ask yourself what in you needs to die in order to receive the message of the Son of Man to the angel of your church." Pause, then complete reading through vs. 19. Pause. Then say, "When you are ready, begin to write what the Son of Man/Human Being says to the angel of your church."
14. When all are through writing, do a guided meditation. "Visualize the one like a Human Being walking in the midst of your church, seeing everything. See his supernal light filling every corner of the buildings, every cell of each person. See it bathed in divine light. Visualize that light becoming more and more intense, transforming the whole church. Trust that God can actually bring this miracle about. Trust God for it in advance, and begin to live out of this vision. Let go of all responsibility to change your church yourself. Praise God for bringing it about. Amen."
15. Share letters to the angel and anything else people wish to share, again seeking common threads or the authentic word of God to the congregation.

(This would take two full sessions at least, with the sharing in #12 and #15. Without them, 2-2.5 hours if you hustle. For background reading, see "The Angels of the Churches," chapter 3 in *Unmasking the Powers*).

On Nonviolence (Records ¶ 371; Parallels 26—Matt. 5:38-41/ Luke 6:29)[4]

1. What negative feelings do you have about this advice?
2. An eye for an eye took the place of what? This principle of proportionate revenge is one of the great human achievements of all time, and serves as basis of all legal codes even today ("Let the punishment fit the crime"). What is meant by the "But I say" here? Is this principle being annulled, or what?

3. Did Jesus "resist" evil? "Resist" here (*antistēnai*) may mean *resist violently*, rise up against someone in war or revolt; that at least is how it is most frequently used in the Greek Old Testament and Josephus. How might that change the meaning of "resist not evil"?[4]

4. Have two people role play striking each other. How will the "aggressor" strike the *right* cheek? He can't use the left arm; that was reserved for unclean tasks. It would have to be with the back of the right hand. Who gives the back of the hand to whom and why? Now have the person struck turn the other cheek. Can the aggressor backhand him again? What happens if he uses his fist? What is the message the victim is giving by turning the cheek?

5. What is Jesus trying to get his hearers ("If anyone strikes *you*") to do? Is this passivity?

6. Vs. 40. People then wore only an outer garment and an undergarment, nothing more. If you give both your garments, what are you doing?

7. Look at Exod. 22:25-27; Deut. 24:10-13. What did the law require?

8. Why was indebtedness such a massive social problem in Palestine? What strategy does Jesus suggest for dealing with it here?

9. In Judaism, nakedness was taboo, and the one who *beheld* it was placed under a curse in Gen. 9:20-27. What does that add to the picture?

10. Role play. (Set this up in advance by having a male participant arrive with jogging shorts or a swimsuit on under his pants; he will be the debtor. Then select an unsuspecting person to be the creditor, and you yourself play the judge. Prepare the debtor beforehand so that he begins by being apologetic at being unable to pay up. As the judge, award the creditor the debtor's coat when he can't pay, and remind her of her legal obligation to return it each night. Then the debtor bridles, becomes indignant, and does his "strip tease," down to nothing but the swimsuit. It's great fun!)

11. Jesus' hearers are the poor ("If anyone sues *you* in

court"), who are used to being subjected to this indignity. What is Jesus trying to get them to do?

12. Read the TEV ("Good News" version) of vs. 41. Roman law provided that soldiers could impress civilians to carry their packs one mile and no further, and any soldier who violated that law was liable to punishment (anywhere from flogging to a reprimand). Why then is Jesus suggesting that his hearers should go a second mile? What position are they putting the soldier in?

13. These sayings have traditionally been interpreted as meaning, "Give in to evil." Abandon all concern for personal justice. Be a doormat for Jesus. Do you see any new possibilities for interpretation now?

14. What does "violent resistance" do for evil? How might we apply Jesus' way of nonviolent resistance to (a) alcoholism, (b) cancer, (c) our own inner shadow, (d) the arms race?

15. If everyone who had heard Jesus say these things began to behave in these *and similar* ways, what would have been the socio-political consequences? How do these teachings relate to Jesus' assertion that the Reign of God was already breaking into their midst? What in your own life have you been "violently resisting" that might be more creatively faced by Jesus' way of nonviolent confrontation?

16. What happens when these sayings are treated as laws instead of "for instances"? Jesus' examples were for unequal relationships. Do they apply to relationships between peers, such as schoolyard fistfights? Bullies?

17. Subdivide into groups of three. One person plays the role of a battered woman, one is a counselor at a shelter for battered women who was formerly a battered spouse herself, and one is an observer. Imagine that the battered woman has been in counseling with you now for some months, and the issue of "what the Bible says" has come up. When she had finally gone to her pastor about her situation, he had told her that the husband is the head of the wife, and that she must go back again and again and turn the other cheek. How will you, the counselor, help

her deal with this belief? After 10-20 minutes, stop and debrief, beginning with the observer's comments. Be sure everyone carefully de-roles; a certain percentage of every group has been or is being battered. You might suggest that anyone who has been battered take one of the other roles.

18. These teachings were the basis for the nonviolent direct action campaigns of Gandhi and Martin Luther King, Jr. Where else are these methods being used today?

19. Cover a long table with butcher paper or newsprint or a paper tablecloth. Place magic markers on it, and have the group circle the table. (With a large group, the leader can put the paper along a wall and do the writing for the group.) Make a timeline beginning on the extreme left with the first known act of civil disobedience—the refusal of the Hebrew midwives to kill the Hebrew babies—and have the group continue filling it with all the nonviolent acts that people can think of right up to the present moment. (These acts have been suppressed in our history books by and large. People will be amazed that there have been so many nonviolent acts in history.)

NOTE: My questions for most of these sections are based on those used by Elizabeth Boyden Howes and other leaders at the Guild for Psychological Studies, as theirs in turn are based on Henry Burton Sharman's. I have in turn modified them, and students of mine have in turn modified mine. I have long waited to acknowledge my appreciation to these students and colleagues who, among others, have taught their teacher so much on the specific passages treated in this chapter:

Al Brock	Will Kniseley
Hal Childs	Constance McClellan
Shirley Cloyes	Ron McDonald
Harvey Cohen	Ted Miller
Jerrold Cunningham	Jay Mitchell
Sarah Darter	Karen Pohlig
Kathryn DeLawter	Sharon Ringe
Susan King Gertmenian	Mary Rose
Al Gilburg	Mary Salsbury
Marta Green	Peg Stern
Peter Hawkins	Scott Summerville
Ellis Johnson	Fred Taylor
Cheryl Johnson Nielsen	Caroline Usher
Steve Goldstein	Ron Whyte
	Christopher Wilke

Above all, I am profoundly grateful to my own teacher and guide, Dr. Howes, to whom I am indebted not just for this approach, but for pointing the way toward my own transformation.

Afterword

This manual alone cannot possibly achieve its stated purpose: to train people in this mode of encountering Scripture. This approach is far more difficult than it appears. To become truly competent as a leader, exposure to the leadership of others more experienced is indispensable. My own hope would be that some of you will discover your vocation in this work, for I am convinced that no more profound means for helping people be transformed is available. As in every true vocation, arduous preparation, training, and apprenticeship are essential. We have too many blind spots simply to go it alone. If you wish to explore further, I would urgently recommend attendance at a workshop or seminar.

For information regarding seminars and training programs with the Guild for Psychological Studies, write 2230 Divisadero Street, San Francisco, CA 94115.

For information regarding workshops with Walter and June Keener-Wink, write Auburn Theological Seminary, 3041 Broadway, New York, N.Y. 10027.

On Miracles

Scholars have been as dogmatic about what could *not* have happened as fundamentalists have been about what *must* have happened. The fact is that historians cannot say whether miracles happened or not. Miracles, as Hume should have taught us long ago, are unique, unprecedented, extraordinary events; they are inaccessible to historical judgments since such judgments can only be made on the basis of analogy from experience. Since miracles by definition have few or no analogies, the historian must remain mute before claims made for such events. Historians still can demand that adequate warrents or evidence be produced for believing that something unusual has happened; they can demonstrate how legendary elements have infiltrated the account (*if* there are parallel versions in which they are missing; otherwise it is largely guesswork). They can provide invaluable checks on superstition by casting a critical eye on extraordinary claims that have a tendentious bent. But to go beyond this to dogmatic assertions that faith healing, or clairvoyance, or resuscitation of the dead is impossible, is to go beyond one's competence as a historian to the faith assertions of a person caught in the narrow confines of a particular world view—or what Paul Ricoeur has called "the available believable."

Let me illustrate. In the 1920s, books by critical scholars on the healing stories in the Gospels tended to say something like this: "Faith healing is impossible, since it would violate the laws of nature. Therefore the healing narratives are legends developed to glorify Jesus as the Christ." At the same time these books were being written, however, psychosomatic medicine was coming into its own, so that by the forties and fifties we were getting books that said something like this: "Psychosomatic healing is possible; therefore Jesus could have healed psychosomatic illnesses. All other healings ascribed to him are legends developed to glorify Jesus as the

Christ." Now we are getting the solid results of scientific studies on the placebo effect, faith healing, ESP, and the powers of the mind, and what seemed "impossible" only five years ago is now regarded by increasing numbers of competent researchers as within the realm of possibility. What has happened here? We have received not one shred of new evidence from the first century. What has changed is our conception of what is possible, on analogy with contemporary experience. The "available believable" has shifted, and with it, historians' judgments.

We cannot but be children of our age. For this reason it would be far more honest for historians (and we are all historians when we approach these texts) to suspend judgments about what is possible and speak only within their competence. A historian can show, for instance, that Matthew has *heightened* the miracle of the healing of Jairus' daughter (Matt. 9:18-26) when he declares her dead at the outset of the story, rather than merely being at the point of death, as in Mark and Luke; but the historian cannot say whether her healing (whatever her state) actually occurred. A humble agnosticism is the only honest stance—whether the historian is a Christian or an atheist. Anything more comes not from the data but from prejudice.

When I work with a miracle story, consequently, I follow Elizabeth Howes' advice and have the group list all the possibilities for accounting for the story, *whether they believe them or not.* Take, for example, Jesus' walking on the water (Mark 6:45-52 par.). The group might come up with a list like this:

1. Jesus really walked on the water.
2. He was walking on a sandbar, or on the shore, and they only thought he was on the sea.
3. The disciples hallucinated.
4. They saw him in a vision.
5. The story was a dream that was taken literally.
6. The story was based on a real event but developed into a legend.

7. The story is one of a resurrection appearance of Jesus projected back into his lifetime.
8. The story is a symbolic tale.

Perhaps even more might be added. Now people are free to take their pick, but I never linger on the question, What *really* happened? because *no one can know*. We must acknowledge, in all honesty, that we cannot say what happened in these stories. Anything beyond that comes of faith: faith that it could not happen, if one is a certain type of believer; faith that it had to have happened, if one is another kind of believer; or faith that it is a symbolic story, if one is another kind of believer, and so on. It is far more candid to list the possibilities and go right on to the question, Whatever happened, what does this story *mean?* than to pretend to know when we do not know.

On Parables

Parables are tiny bits of coal squeezed into diamonds, condensed metaphors that catch the ray of something ultimate and glint it at our lives. Parables are not illustrations; they do not support, elaborate, or simplify a more basic idea. They are not ideas at all, nor can they ever be reduced to theological statements. They are the jeweled portals of another world; we cannot see through them like windows, but lights are refracted through their surfaces that would otherwise blind us—or pass unseen.

Parables participate in the reality which they communicate. There is a "simultaneity of the moment of insight and the choice of metaphor—they appear to come together and be forever wedded."[1] Nor can parables ever be exhausted; they are always more than we can tell. They are the precipitate of something ineffable; they percolate up from depths wherein the Kingdom itself is working its ineluctable work. They come from the same energizing reality that causes the seeds to germinate and the leaven to rise. They rise with the leaven.

Parables have suffered under the rationalism and idealist orientation of biblical scholars ever since Jülicher uttered his dictum in 1886 that every parable has one and only one central point. Jülicher was of course trying to break the back of allegorizing, which attempts to impose a set theological meaning upon every parabolic detail. Allegorizing uses equal signs: in the parable of the ten maidens, for example, the bridegroom = Jesus, his delay = the overdue second coming, the wedding = the Kingdom, the shut door = the last judgment, the wise maidens = the true believers, the foolish maidens = the backsliders, and so forth. (See pp. 133-34.)

Unfortunately, Jülicher merely substituted for an allegorizing of the parts an allegorizing of the whole. In this he has been followed by almost every commentator until recent times.[2] The reduction of every parable to a single point (read: *idea*) renders it a mere illustration of more primary theological meanings. Lost is all sense of the parable's artistic integrity, its capacity to tell us something we do not know and could not come by in any other way, its ability to evoke experiences we have never had, and an awareness of realities not even guessed at before.

"Allegorizing" should be distinguished from allegory in the same way that "psychologizing" must be distinguished from psychology. Allegorizing is a kind of reductionism. It shows its hand when details intended literally are invested with inappropriate metaphorical weight—when, for example, the ass, inn, or Jericho in the parable of the compassionate Samaritan is made into a matter of deep mystical import. Or it may take the form of an intellectualism that has lost all sense of the feeling tone of the figure, and seeks to reduce the multiple meanings of a parable to just one, which is then regarded as normative and correct. Or allegorizing can involve applying a parable to a situation that it simply does not fit, or stretching the metaphor beyond its limits.

Allegory, in distinction from allegorizing, is as valid a literary device as parable, but is not, as has long been supposed, a form at all. It is, as Madeleine Boucher has pointed out, simply a device of meaning, an extended metaphor in narrative form. The prodigal son, the friend at midnight, and the unmerciful servant are allegories, she believes, but they are no less authentic bearers of the mystery of God's Reign than other figurative modes of expression.

A parable (or a simile, allegory, exemplary story, or any other figure) stands in an intermediate position between the known and the unknown. Valid interpretation presses through the metaphor to the unknown; allegorizing rebounds back to the safety of the known. In valid interpretation we feel our way into each symbol in order to sense the surplus of meaning that beckons us beyond ourselves to discover something new. In allegorizing we equate each symbol with something we already know, and render the parable's meaning by a theological paraphrase. Valid interpretation is a listening to what can otherwise not be heard without the parable; allegorizing is a speech imposed on the parable which tells it what it must mean. In the final analysis, then, allegorizing is an attitude of domination over the text and satisfaction with what one already has. It is a subtle or blatant form of arrogance. It is the death of interpretation.

To hear a parable, then, means to submit oneself to entering its world, to make oneself vulnerable, to know that we do not know at the outset what it means. Parables function much as the Zen *koan*, or the tales of the dervishes, to tease the mind out of familiar channels and into a more right-brain view of things. Parables have hooks all over them; they can grab each of us in a different way, according to our need. Are we discouraged about our ministry and its meager results? Then we can identify with the sower and look with new hope toward an unprecedented harvest. Have we unwittingly filled our lives with activities, cares, false loves which threaten to choke off the ultimate values to which we once so flamingly committed ourselves? We might then see ourselves as thorn-infested soil. Are we just grazing the surface, dabbling in the life of the spirit, halfheartedly dipping into the struggle for a just and humane world? Are we perhaps the rocky soil? Or have we become stupefied by dogma, or our own vaunted pride in reason so that we can hear nothing new? Have our paths become ruts? This is but a skimming of meanings I have heard people find in this puzzling and inexhaustible riddle. (The parable of the sower—see pp. 128-29.)

The fallacy of the one-point theory should have become manifest the moment it became clear that scholars themselves could not agree on what the one point was—though each was certain that *he* knew! The fact is that there is no one point of entry into these parables, and no single exit. That is precisely why they are so timeless, so universally potent, so masterful. Like fire-seeking rockets for air-to-air combat, they seek us out and they find us. The contradictions in the interpretation of the parable of the sower (see p. 129) are proof of this. The early preachers in the Christian community tried to fix the "one" meaning of the parable by providing a definitive interpretation. But they too could not agree, some seeing the seed as the word (vs. 14) and the people as the soil (vs. 15b), others seeing the people as seed (vss. 15, 16, 18, 20). They would have mastered the parable, but it overpowered them and made nonsense of their attempt.

Many of us, still shackled by the chains of rationalistic exegesis, approach a parable fairly confident that we "know what it's about." All the more important then that we find ways to *de-familiarize* the parable, to see it from new angles, to open new possibilities for hearing, as Jesus repeatedly warns us to do. Critical insights can sometimes help. So can identifying with various aspects of the parable, gestalting it from many angles, or miming it. As a leader you will probably have to work hard to keep people from allegorizing it piece by piece or reducing it to a single bland "I know just what it means, it means this" statement. Get them to *feel* into the symbols, to experience its mystery, its near numinosity, until they begin to sense that they do not understand it after all, but that possibly—it understands them.

On Psychologizing

Some people, not familiar with the "psychologism" debate,[1] mistakenly assume that it is "psychologizing" to use psychological insights in any form for exegesis. But psychologizing refers technically only to instances in which meaning or motivation is inferred from inadequate data or read into the text, or where the content of a passage is reduced to nothing but its psychodynamics. In fact, virtually every narrative requires psychological analysis to be understood: *why* did she do this? or why did he say that? Psychology is merely one among all the tools that historiography, as a field-encompassing field, gratefully employs. The analysis of the function of archetypes and symbols in texts by Jung and Howes is merely an extension of this mode of inquiry on the basis of new insights into the nature of psyche, symbol, and myth.

It would be psychologizing, for example, to inquire into Mary's feelings as reflected in the Magnificat (Luke 1:46-55), if on critical grounds we suspect that her hymn was composed by others. But we can legitimately ask what feelings those anonymous but exulting "others" are expressing.

It would be psychologizing to develop from the Jacob saga in Genesis a personality profile of the man Jacob. We simply cannot know to what extent legend and folk memory have colored or even created the traditions. We can legitimately inquire, however, into the psychological dynamics of the story *as we find it.* Here we are asking, not about Jacob, but the intentions of the storytellers: what they intend their hearers to understand, and how the story is designed to move the hearers.[2]

It would be psychologizing to argue, on the basis of Jesus' use of "Abba" ("Daddy") as a metaphor for God, that he had an Oedipal complex, or was perhaps a bastard who was compensating for not knowing his earthly father. Such questions are illegitimate, not because they are offensive, but because there simply is not enough data even to begin an inquiry. It *is* legitimate, however, to ask what the term "Abba" meant for Jesus, what role that symbol played in Israel, and what it might mean to be in touch with the reality to which this metaphor points.

The hazards of psychologizing are not to be minimized. One sees it constantly among certain "psychohistorians." Two particularly egregious examples are studies by Dan O. Via, Jr. ("The Prodigal Son: A Jungian Reading") and Mary Ann Tolbert ("The Prodigal Son: An Essay in Literary Criticism from a Psychoanalytic Perspective") both in *Semeia* 9 (1977), 1-44. Both authors impose psychological theory on the text. The structure of Jungian (Via) or Freudian (Tolbert) psychology is made normative, and the text merely fitted in. This allegorizes the text; it becomes a mere illustration of a particular psychological theory. After the theory has become clear, the parable is expendable. In the process the parable has lost all religious reference and has become nothing more than a crude anticipation of insights now given systematic articulation by modern psychology.

The point of using psychological insights in studying biblical texts is not to prove that the Bible is somehow "relevant" because it says what any astute psychologist already knows. Nor is it to legitimate psychology by appeal to the still redoubtable authority of Scripture. Psychological insights simply are drawn on where appropriate—and that is determined by the nature of the text, not by psychological theory.

The application of psychological insights and exercises *to ourselves* as a means of appropriating the text is one of the particular contributions of Elizabeth Howes. Here elements of the story, which have now taken on an *objective* reality through the critical amplification of the text, act as interior probes into *us*. This is as far from psychologizing as one could possibly get. *Not the text, but we ourselves are the object of analysis,* and it is precisely the objectivity of the text, its very alienness and opposition to us, which is most able to help us discover those aspects of ourselves lost to consciousness and allowed to languish in the dungeons of the soul.

Howes has taken this process even one step further, to an analysis of how Jesus worked with and related to the achetypal images alive in him and the world of his day. Jung identified the man Jesus and the Christ of faith. Howes and her associates do not begin seminars with the assumption that Jesus was the Christ, but rather raise the question of Jesus' relationship to the messianic image. In so doing they open an alternative route to religious consciousness, one that moves not through the Christian myth but through what Jesus did with his own myth. This is not Jesuolatry or old-style Harnack "liberalism." It is a genuinely new avenue of approach, deserving of serious reflection. Dr. Howes has developed these insights in her book, *Jesus' Answer to God* (San Francisco: Guild for Psychological Studies Publishing House, 2230 Divisadero, San Francisco, CA 94115, 1984).

Notes

Preface to the Second Edition

1. See the author's article "How I Have Been Snagged by the Seat of My Pants While Reading the Bible," *Christian Century* 92 (September 24, 1975), pp. 816-19.

1. Transformed by the Renewal of Our Minds

1. Michael S. Gazzaniga, "The Split Brain of Man," in Robert E. Ornstein, *The Nature of Human Consciousness* (San Francisco: W. H. Freeman, 1973), pp. 91, 92. This volume of collected essays, plus Ornstein's *The Psychology of Consciousness* (New York: Viking Press, 1972), Kenneth Pelletier's *Toward a Science of Consciousness* (New York: Delta, 1978), and Eugene P. Wratchford's *Brain Research and Personhood: A Philosophical and Theological Inquiry* (Washington, D. C.: University Press of America, 1979) provide an excellent introduction to this exciting new field. Data for what follows and for Fig. 1 have been taken from these and other sources referred to in subsequent notes.

2. Sally P. Springer and Georg Deutsch, *Left Brain, Right Brain*, Revised Edition (New York: W. H. Freeman and Co., 1985), p. 272.

3. Eran Zaidel, "Implications: Introduction," in *The Dual Brain: Hemispheric Specialization in Humans*, ed. D. Frank Benson and Zaidel (New York: Guilford Press, 1985), pp. 310-15. See also Roger W. Sperry, "Consciousness, Personal Identity, and the Divided Brain," in *The Dual Brain*, pp. 17-18: The right hemisphere specializes in fitting forms into molds, judging a whole circle's size from a part of its arc, grouping different sized and shaped blocks into categories, perceiving whole plane forms from a collection of parts, and intuiting geometric properties. He is critical of popularizers who have extrapolated from such facts to localizing intuition, the unconscious, parapsychological sensitivity, Eastern philosophy, hypnotic sensibility, altered states of consciousness, etc., in the right hemisphere. They may indeed prove to be localized there, he says, but it will take years to determine if this is so. And there are, besides laterality, front-to-back and different hierarchical and organizational levels in the brain as well, and these also must be accounted for.

4. I need to stress "*most* involved," because art generally does *not* seem to be localized simply in the right brain. Some victims of right hemisphere stroke (but not the majority) are still musical, and others, suffering from left hemisphere lesions, become unmusical. There is no clear pattern for artists either. Poets and writers, however, are incapacitated by left hemisphere lesions (Avraham Schweiger, "Harmony of the Spheres and the Hemispheres: The Arts and Hemispheric Specialization," in *The Dual Brain*, pp. 359-73). The right brain, however, does seem to play a decisive role in both artistic production and appreciation. Isabelle Peretz and José Morais conclude that whereas music may not be localized in the right brain,

subcomponents of functions are clearly dominant there. Combinations of melody and rhythm patterns are better handled by the right hemisphere in non-musically trained subjects, whereas trained musicians showed clear left-hemisphere dominance, but only when literate and trained in Western tonal music. With Eastern or atonal music they were no different than the right hemisphere-dominant untrained nonmusicians or illiterate musicians ("Determinants for Laterality for Music: Towards an Information Processing Account," in *Handbook of Dichotic Listening: Theory, Methods and Research*, ed. Kenneth Hugdahl [Chichester: John Wiley & Sons, 1988], pp. 232-51).

5. Pelletier, *Toward a Science of Consciousness*, pp. 91, 97-100.

6. Betty Edwards, *Drawing on the Right Side of the Brain* (New York: St. Martin's Press, 1979), p. 31.

7. Pelletier, *Toward a Science of Consciousness*, pp. 93-94.

8. Thomas G. Bever and Robert J. Chiarello, "Cerebral Dominance in Musicians and Nonmusicians," *Science*, 185 (Aug. 9, 1974): pp. 537-39.

9. Mountcastle, in Pelletier, *Toward a Science of Consciousness*, p. 96.

10. Roger M. Williams, "Why Adults Should Draw," *Saturday Review*, Sept. 3, 1977, pp. 11-16.

11. Pelletier, *Toward a Science of Consciousness*, p. 105.

12. Eugene G. d'Aquili and Charles Laughlin, Jr., "The Biopsychological Determinants of Religious Ritual Behavior," *Zygon*, 10 (1975): pp. 32-58. So also, independently, Pelletier, *Toward a Science of Consciousness*, p. 110; see also E. Gellhorn, M.D., and W. F. Kiely, M.D., "Mystical States of Consciousness: Neurophysiological and Clinical Aspects," *The Journal of Nervous and Mental Disease*, 154 (1972): pp. 399-405.

13. See chap. 6 of Jung's *Memories, Dreams and Reflections* (New York: Vintage Books, 1965). On the evolutionary potential of a shift to an integral approach to reality, see Jean Gebser, *The Ever-Present Origin* (Athens, OH: Ohio University Press, 1985).

14. Recent applications of holographic theory suggest that the whole brain is far more active as a total entity than some attempts at localizing brain activity have taken into account (Pelletier, *Toward a Science of Consciousness*, chap. 4). Barbara W. Lef's caution is worthy of regard: "The nervous system is an interactive, interconnected, immensely complex structure, and therefore emphasis on any single subsystem is useful only as a convenient heuristic. Underlying any behaviour is the action of a nervous system functioning in concert, not in discrete segments." ("Neurological Bases of Revitalization Movements," *Zygon*, 13 [1978]: p. 282). See additionally the entire issue of *Scientific American*, 241 (Sept., 1979), *Psychology Abstracts* (under "commissuratomy"), and back issues of *Brain/Mind Bulletin*. James Ashbrook and Paul Walaskay explored the theme theologically in *Christianity for Pious Skeptics* (Nashville: Abingdon, 1977) and elsewhere.

For a more cautious assessment of the whole field, see Howard Gardner, "What we know (and don't know) about the two halves of the brain," *Harvard Magazine*, 80 (March-April, 1978): pp. 24-27.

While new information will undoubtedly lead to the modification of present knowledge in this field, it is not likely to challenge the recognition that the human brain operates in at least two discrete cognitive modes, however intricate their interrelations.

In addition to newer sources already noted, see David Ottoson, *Duality and Unity of the Brain: Unified Functioning and Specialization of the Hemispheres*

Notes

(New York: Plenum Press, 1987); A. Glass, *Individual Differences in Hemisphere Specialization* (New York: Plenum Press, 1984); Anne Harrington, *Medicine, Mind, and the Double Brain* (Princeton: Princeton University Press, 1987); N. Geschwind and A. M. Galaburda, eds., *Cerebral Dominance* (Cambridge: Harvard University Press, 1984); Vsevolod L. Bianchi, *The Right and Left Hemispheres of the Animal Brain* (New York: Gordon and Breach Science Publishers, 1988); Alan Beaton, *Left Side, Right Side: A Review of Laterality Research* (New Haven: Yale University Press, 1985).

15. "Since the right hemisphere deals more effectively with complex patterns taken as a whole than with individual parts taken serially, its mode of expression is most often in the form of 'word pictures' such as metaphors, puns, double entendres, and rebuses. Elements of these verbal constructions do not have fixed definitions but depend on context, and can shift in meaning when seen as parts of a new pattern." (Pelletier, *Toward a Science of Consciousness*, p. 102, citing the work of David Galin).

16. M. S. Gazzaniga and J. E. LeDoux, *The Integrated Mind* (New York: Plenum Press, 1978); cited by Springer and Deutsch, *Left Brain, Right Brain*, pp. 263-64, italics mine.

17. Ornstein, *The Psychology of Consciousness*, p. 139.

2. Introducing This Approach

1. The best arrangement of the Synoptic Gospels continues to be that of Henry Burton Sharman, *The Records of the Life of Jesus*, 1917, available in a new edition using the Revised Standard Version, from the Guild for Psychological Studies Publishing House, 2230 Divisadero, San Francisco, CA 94115. Also available, though not so clearly organized, is *Gospel Parallels* (New York: Thomas Nelson & Sons, 1949), using the RSV but following the arrangement of Huck's Greek synopsis of 1892 (9th ed. by Hans Lietzmann, 1936).

2. "The Seminar Method Used by The Guild for Psychological Studies," 1976, privately published by The Guild for Psychological Studies, 2230 Divisadero, San Francisco, CA 94115. See also "After Thirty Years: The History and Purpose of The Guild for Psychological Studies," 1973, from the same source.

3. A Seminar Revisited

1. Sharman, *The Records of the Life of Jesus*, ¶ 37 L-R; *Gospel Parallels*, ¶ 27.

2. This comment sounds very hopeless. Actually, the speaker would not have said it in this context unless she were already entertaining the need to change. By articulating her resistance she is testing it to see how strong it really is. The exercises that accompany the next two texts are indispensable for giving her a chance to experiment with actually letting go of her need for the enemy. To have ended without the exercises would have left her confirmed in her hopelessness.

3. Many of us have become so "familiar" with Jesus' teaching that we fail to see how radical it is. This person's comment could have stopped any further discussion of this point dead in its tracks. The leader's task here is to help the group hold on to the speaker's positive affirmation and at the same time

169

explore the stunning claim made about God—a claim which, as we see shortly, is in fact a considerable problem for our society—and, unconsciously, for most of us.

4. *Records* ¶ 38F-I; *Parallels* ¶ 36. The dialogue for this section and the next is based on a transcript from a Hartford Seminary Foundation evening series, Spring 1979, with additions from an Auburn Seminary workshop, April, 1979, and notes from Four Springs.

5. *Records* ¶ 37A; *Parallels* ¶ 22.

6. I was not able to understand why Elizabeth Howes stressed the importance of the "altar" until once in a group I skipped the questions dealing with it. In the feedback after the exercise I discovered that almost no one had been able to work through the reconciliation in the imaginary dialogues they had done with persons from whom they were estranged. Without the central value represented by the altar they were not able to believe in the possibility of the miracle of reconciliation; and without that central value they also tended to indulge themselves in the hopelessness of doing anything about it.

4. Leading a Group

1. I use "revolutionary" with full seriousness. Ernesto Cardinal helped foment revolution in Nicaragua by using just such a style of Bible study to raise consciousness about the economic and political oppression of the Somoza regime (see Bibliography).

6. Developing and Using Questions

1. Elizabeth Boyden Howes, "After Thirty Years: The History and Purpose of the Guild for Psychological Studies" (San Francisco: Guild for Psychological Studies, 1973), p. 6.

7. Introducing Biblical Criticism

1. Harvey, *The Historian and the Believer* (New York: Macmillan, 1966), p. 281.

8. Engaging the Other Side of the Brain

1. Constance Holden, "Paul MacLean and the Triune Brain," *Science,* 204 (July, 1979): p. 1068. MacLean believes that the emotions involve not just the right cerebellum, but the lower brain centers as well.

2. Edwards, *Drawing on the Right Side of the Brain*, p. 42. Her drawing exercises provide experimental proof of the utility of split-brain theory.

3. I have developed this particular example at length in "Wrestling with God: The Use of Psychological Insights in Biblical Study," *Religion in Life,* XLVII (1978): pp. 136-47.

4. Moon, *Joseph's Son* (Francistown, N. H.: The Golden Quill Press, 1972); also available from the Guild for Psychological Studies.

9. Sample Questions on Biblical Texts

1. See Appendix 2 for the rationale for identifying with various aspects of the parable rather than seeking its "one" meaning.

2. God's Reign is not mentioned in the parable, but it is in a block of parables about God's reign, uses the same image (seed) and structure (a growth process from small to great) as the others, and participates in the same reality that evoked them. Mark 4:11 par. in any case specifically identifies it as a parable about God's Reign. It is probably, more precisely, a parable about how to hear a parable about God's Reign.

3. See Appendix 2.

4. For exegetical background, see the author's *Violence and Nonviolence in South Africa* (Philadelphia: New Society Publishers, 1987), chapter 2.

Appendix 2

1. Sallie McFague TeSelle, *Speaking in Parables* (Philadelphia: Fortress Press, 1975), p. 45.

2. For a healthy corrective see John Dominic Crossan, *In Parables* (New York: Harper & Row, 1973); Madeleine Boucher, *The Mysterious Parable* (Washington, D. C.: Catholic Biblical Association of America, 1977); and TeSelle.

Appendix 3

1. See Nicola Abbagnano, "Psychologism," *Encyclopedia of Philosophy*, ed. Paul Edwards (New York: Macmillan, 1967), VI, 520 ff.

2. See the author's "On Wrestling with God. The Use of Psychological Insights in Biblical Study," *Religion in Life*, XLVII (1978): pp. 136-47.

Selected Bibliography

Essential Reference Works on the Synoptic Gospels

This brief list of reference works is provided in response to frequent requests from laity and clergy who have no access to theological libraries and have limited funds for purchasing books. Some of them are available in paperback.

A book on New Testament introduction:

Kümmel, W. G. *Introduction to the New Testament,* rev. ed. Nashville: Abingdon Press, 1975. This is the most exhaustive, scholarly, and reliable introduction; it may also be a little overwhelming.

More readable are:

Bornkamm, Gunther, *The New Testament: A Guide to Its Writing.* London: S.P.C.K., 1974. Perhaps the clearest and easiest for the general reader.

Pheme Perkins, *Reading the New Testament* (Ramsey, NJ: Paulist Press, 1988).

Davies, W. D. *Invitation to the New Testament.* Garden City, N.Y.: Doubleday, 1966.

Fuller, Reginald H. *A Critical Introduction to the New Testament.* London: Gerald Duckworth, 1966.

Marxsen, Willi. *Introduction to the New Testament.* Philadelphia: Fortress Press, 1968.

Perrin, Norman. *Introduction to the New Testament.* New York: Harcourt Brace Jovanovich, 1974.

The New Oxford Annotated Bible with Apocrypha, Expanded Edition, Revised Standard Version. New York: Oxford University Press, 1977. The useful notes provide a running commentary and often a quick answer to questions raised in the group. Also has maps in the back.

A Bible Dictionary:

The Interpreters Dictionary of the Bible. 4 vols. plus
Supplement. Nashville: Abingdon Press, 1962 and 1976.
The best, but it is expensive.

Another good but cheaper one-volume edition is:

Harper's Bible Dictionary by Madeleine S. Miller and J. Lane
Miller. New York: Harper and Bros., 1952.

A one-volume commentary on the whole Bible:

The Jerome Biblical Commentary, second edition, ed.
Raymond E. Brown *et al.* Englewood Cliffs, N.J.:
Prentice-Hall, 1989.
Harper's Bible Commentary, ed. James L. Mays. San
Francisco: Harper & Row, 1988.
The Interpreter's One-Volume Commentary on the Bible, ed.
Charles M. Laymon. Nashville: Abingdon Press, 1971.
Peake's Commentary on the Bible, new edition, ed. Matthew
Black and H. H. Rowley. New York: Thomas Nelson &
Sons, 1962.

A concordance:

Young, Robert. *Analytical Concordance to the Holy Bible.*
London: Lutterworth Press (1879), 1952.
Morrison, Clinton. *An Analytical Concordance to the Revised
Standard Version of the New Testament.* Philadelphia:
Westminster Press, 1979.

Single-book commentaries on the Gospels: I have been most
helped by:

Myers, Ched. *Binding the Strong Man: A Political Reading of
Mark's Story of Jesus.* Maryknoll, NY: Orbis Press, 1988.
Nineham, D. E. *The Gospel of St. Mark* (Pelican Gospel
Commentaries). New York: Penguin Books, 1963.

Schweizer, Eduard. *St. Matthew*. London: S.P.C.K. 1976.

———. *St. Mark*. Richmond: John Knox Press, 1970.

———. *St. Luke*. Louisville: John Knox Westminister, 1984.

Conzelmann, Hans. *The Theology of St. Luke*. New York: Harper and Bros., 1961. Use the Index to find the passages you are working on.

On the teaching of Jesus:

Jeremias, Joachim. *New Testament Theology*. New York: Charles Scribner's Sons, 1970. A masterpiece. Use it like a commentary by referring to the Index.

Borg, Marcus. *Jesus: A New Vision*. San Francisco: Harper and Row, 1988.

Bornkamm, Gunther. *Jesus of Nazareth*. New York: Harper and Bros., 1960.

On Jesus' parables:

Scott, Bernard Brandon. *Hear Then the Parable*. Minneapolis: Augsburg Fortress, 1989.

Crossan, John Dominic. *In Parables*. New York: Harper & Row, 1973.

Jeremias, Joachim. *The Parables of Jesus*, rev. ed. New York: Charles Scribner's Sons, 1969.

On the period:

Jeremias, Joachim. *Jerusalem in the Time of Jesus*. New York: Charles Scribner's Sons, 1969.

Lohse, Eduard. *The New Testament Environment*. Nashville: Abingdon, 1976.

Titles Related to This Approach:

Howes, Elizabeth Boyden. *Intersection and Beyond*. 1971. The Guild for Psychological Studies, 2230 Divisadero St., San Francisco, CA 94115.

———. and Moon, Sheila. *The Choicemaker*. Wheaton, Ill.: Theosophical Press, 1973.

———. "After Thirty Years: The History and Purpose of the Guild for Psychological Studies," 1973, from the Guild office (above).

Wink, Walter. *The Bible in Human Transformation*. Philadelphia: Fortress Press, 1973.

———. "Wrestling with God: Using Psychological Insights in Biblical Study," *Religion in Life,* XLVII (1978), pp. 136-47.

———. "The Parable of the Compassionate Samaritan," *Review and Expositor,* LXXVI (1979): pp. 199-218.

———. "Interpretation—A Retrospective," *Auburn News,* Spring 1988, 6-7.

Van Ness, Patricia, *Transforming Bible Study with Children* (Nashville: Abingdon Press, 1991).

Dawson, Gerrit Scott with Steven G.P. Strickler, *Living Stories: Creating Incarnational Bible Study for Children* (working title, forthcoming).

Other Bible Study Approaches:

Cardenal, Ernesto. *The Gospel in Solentiname*. Maryknoll, N.Y.: Orbis Books, 1976.

L'Heureux, Conrad E. *Life Journey and the Old Testament: An Experimental Approach to the Bible and Personal Transformation*. New York: Paulist Press, 1986.

Morrison, Mary C. *Approaching the Gospel Together*. Wallingford, PA: Pendle Hill Publications, 1986.

Weber, Hans-Ruedi. *Experiments with Bible Study*. Geneva: World Council of Churches, 1981.

Boomershine, Thomas. *Story Journey: An Invitation to the Gospel as Storytelling*. Nashville: Abingdon, 1988.

Maas, Robin. *The Church Bible Study Handbook*. Nashville: Abingdon, 1982.

Gobbel, A. Roger and Gertrude G. *The Bible: A Child's Playground*. Philadelphia: Fortress Press, 1986.